LETTERS
FROM
A FARMER in *Pennsylvania*,
TO THE INHABITANTS
OF
THE BRITISH COLONIES

BY
JOHN DICKINSON

INTRODUCTION.

In the issue of the PENNSYLVANIA CHRONICLE AND UNIVERSAL ADVERTISER of November 30th-December 3d, 1767, appeared the first of twelve successive weekly "*Letters from a*FARMER *in* Pennsylvania *to the Inhabitants of the* British *Colonies*," in which the attitude assumed by the British Parliament towards the American Colonies was exhaustively discussed. So extensive was their popularity that they were immediately reprinted in almost all our Colonial newspapers.

The outbursts of joy throughout America occasioned by the repeal of the Stamp Act had scarcely subsided when, the protracted illness of Lord Chatham having left the Ministry without a head, the indomitable Charles Townsend, to the amazement of his colleagues and unfeigned delight of his King, introduced measure after measure under the pretence that they were demanded by the necessities of the Exchequer; but in reality for the purpose of demonstrating the supremacy of the power of the Parliament of Great Britain over her colonies in America. Among these Acts were those which provided for the billeting of troops in the various colonies; others[xviii] called for duties upon glass, lead, paint, oil, tea, etc. Of dire portent was the provision therein, that the revenues thus obtained be used for the maintenance of a Civil List in America, and for the payment of the salaries of the Royal Governors and Justices, salaries which had hitherto been voted by the various Assemblies. The Assembly of New York, having failed to comply strictly with the letter of the law in regard to the billeting of the King's troops, was punished by having its legislative powers suspended.

This action boded ill for the future of any law-making body in America which should fail to carry out strictly any measure upon which the British Parliament might agree. The Colonies needed a common ground on which to meet in their opposition to these arbitrary Acts of Parliament. The deeds of violence and the tumultuous and passionate harangues in the northern colonies met with little sympathy among a large class in the middle and southern colonies, who, while chafing under the attacks upon their liberties, hesitated to favor resistance to the home government because of their unswerving loyalty to their King and their love for the country to whom and to which they owed allegiance. To these "The Farmer" appealed when he wrote, "The cause of liberty is a cause of too much dignity to be slighted by turbulence and tumult. It ought to be maintained in a manner suitable[xix] to her nature, those who engage in it should breathe a sedate yet fervent spirit animating them to actions of prudence, justice, modesty, bravery, humanity and magnanimity." The convincing logic of these letters clearly proved that the constitutional rights belonging to Englishmen were being trampled upon in the colonies, and furnished a platform upon which all those who feared their liberties were endangered could unite.

Under the date of the fifth of November, 1767, the seventy-ninth anniversary of the day on which the landing of William the Third at Torbay gave constitutional liberty to all Englishmen, John Dickinson, of Pennsylvania (for before long it became known that he was the illustrious author), in a letter addressed to his "beloved countrymen," called attention to the lack of interest shown by the Colonies in the act suspending the legislative powers of New York, and logically pointed out that the precedent thereby established was a blow at the liberty of all the other Colonies, laying particular emphasis upon the danger of mutual inattention by the Colonies to the interests of one another.

The education and training of the author well qualified him to handle his subject. Born in 1732 on his ancestral plantation on the eastern shore of Maryland, from early youth John Dickinson had had the advantages[xx] of a classical education.[1] His nineteenth year found him reading law in a lawyer's office in Philadelphia. Three years later, he sailed for England, where he devoted four important years to study at the Middle Temple, and then and there obtained that knowledge of English common law and constitutional history, and imbibed the traditions of liberty belonging to Englishmen on which he later founded his plea for the resistance of the Colonies to the ministerial attacks upon their liberty. On his return home he took up the practice of his profession at Philadelphia, and immediately won for himself a high place at the Bar. Elected in 1760 a member of the Assembly of Delaware, his reputation for ability and political discernment gained him its speakership. In 1762 he became a member of the Assembly of Pennsylvania, where he acquired great prominence and unpopularity, which later cost him his seat in that body, on account of his opposition to the Assembly's sending a petition to the King praying that the latter "would *resume* the government of the province, making such compensation to the proprietaries as would be equitable, and permitting the inhabitants to enjoy under the new government the privileges that have been granted to them by and under your Royal ministries."

[xxi]

Possibly Dickinson's knowledge of the personality of the Ministry and the dominant spirits in English political circles gained while abroad, led him bitterly to attack this measure, fathered and supported by Franklin, for subsequent events soon showed the far-sightedness which led him to distrust the wisdom of a demand for the revoking of the Proprietary Charter, even though it were a bad one. His part in the controversy forced even his bitterest opponents to admire his ability. The enormous debt incurred by Great Britain during the then recent war with France led the Ministry to look for some way of lightening taxation at home. It was decided that America must pay a share toward lifting the burden resting heavily on those in England, caused by the financing of the expenses of a war which drove France from North America. The fact that the colonies had furnished, equipped and maintained in the field twenty-five thousand troops and had incurred debts far heavier in proportion than those at home was forgotten. In 1764 was passed the "Sugar Act," which extended and enlarged the Navigation Acts and made England the channel through which not only all European, but also all Asiatic trade to and from the colonies must flow. At the same time an announcement was made that "Stamp Duties" would be added later on. The next year from Dickinson's[xxii] pen appeared a pamphlet entitled "THE LATE REGULATIONS RESPECTING THE BRITISH COLONIES ON THE CONTINENT OF AMERICA CONSIDERED, in a Letter from a Gentleman in PHILADELPHIA to his Friend in LONDON," in which these late regulations and proposed measures were discussed entirely from an economic standpoint. In it was clearly shown how dependent were the manufacturers and traders in England for their prosperity upon the trade of the colonies and that any restraint of American trade would naturally curtail the ability of those in the colonies to purchase from the home market. The Stamp Act was opposed on the ground that the already impoverished colonies would be drained of all their gold and silver which necessarily would have to go abroad in the payment for the stamps. This letter was conciliatory and persuasive, yet in the closing pages Dickinson asked:

"What then can we do? Which way shall we turn ourselves? How may we mitigate the miseries of our country? *Great Britain* gives us an example to guide us? SHE TEACHES US TO MAKE A DISTINCTION BETWEEN HER INTERESTS AND OUR OWN.

"Teaches! She requires—commands—insists upon it—threatens—compels—and even distresses us into it.

"We have our choice of these two things—to continue our present limited and[xxiii]disadvantageous commerce—or to promote manufactures among ourselves, with a habit of economy, and thereby remove the necessity we are now under of being supplied by *Great Britain*.

"It is not difficult to determine which of these things is most eligible. Could the last of them be only so far executed as to bring our demand for British manufactures below the profits of our foreign trade, and the amount of our commodities immediately remitted home, these colonies might revive and flourish. States and families are enriched by the same means; that is, by being so industrious and frugal as to spend less than what they raise can pay for."

The various Non-Importation Agreements signed during the next ten years, bear testimony to the popularity of the proposed plan.

This pamphlet circulated freely and increased Dickinson's reputation as that of a man capable of thoroughly discussing public measures; it also brought his name to the attention of the British public for whom the "Letter" was especially written.

At the call of Massachusetts, representatives of nine of the colonies met in New York in October, 1764, and after a long discussion (in which Dickinson's knowledge of constitutional law and English colonial policy enabled him to assume the leadership) issued a "Declaration of Rights," in[xxiv] which it was asserted that the inhabitants of the Colonies, standing on their rights as Englishmen, could not be taxed by the House of Commons while unrepresented in that body. Memorials were sent abroad protesting against the proposed acts, expressing, however, their willingness to meet loyally as in the past any properly accredited requisitions for funds sent to the various Assemblies. Notwithstanding this opposition, and the protests of all friends of America in England, the Stamp Act was passed. A year later it was repealed.

JUST PUBLISHED.

Printed on a large Type, and fine Paper,
And to be sold at the *LONDON BOOK STORE*
North Side of King-street

LETTERS
FROM
A FARMER in *PENNSYLVANIA*

To the INHABITANTS of the
BRITISH COLONIES.

(Price two Pistareens)

Among all the WRITERS in favor of the COLONIES, the FARMER shines unrivalled, for *strength* of *Argument, Elegance* of *Diction, Knowledge* in the *Laws* of *Great Britain*, and *the true interest* of the COLONIES: A*pathetic* and *persuasive eloquence* runs thro the whole of these Letters: They have been printed in every *Colony* from *Florida* to *Nova Scotia*; and the *universal applause* so justly bestowed on the *AUTHOR*, hath fully testified the GRATITUDE of the PEOPLE OF AMERICA, for such an *able Adviser* and *affectionate Friend.*

Written in a plain, pure style, with illustrations and arguments drawn from ecclesiastical, classical and English history, each point proven with telling accuracy and convincing logic, conciliatory to the English people, and filled with expressions of loyalty to the King, these essays, popularly known as the "Farmer's Letters," furnished the basis on which all those who resented the attacks on their liberty were able to unite. Town meetings[2] and Assemblies vied with each other in their resolutions of thanks. The "Letters" were published immediately in book form in Philadelphia (three different editions), New York, Boston (two different editions), Williamsburgh, London (with a preface written by Franklin), and Dublin.[xxv] [xxvi] Franklin was influential, also, in having them translated into French, and published on the Continent. Owing to the beauty of its typography and the excellence of its book-making, the Boston edition, published by Messrs. Mein & Fleeming, has been selected for republication, and has been reprinted line for line and page for page, in a type varying but slightly from that used by Mein & Fleeming. A few typographical errors have been corrected, but the irregularities in spelling, wherever they exist throughout the various editions, have been retained. The binding also is a reproduction of that of the original. Its publication[3] was announced in the "Boston Chronicle," March 14-21, 1768, by the advertisement reprinted on the preceding page.

Valuable as these "Letters" were at home in uniting all factions in their measures of resistance, yet their influence abroad was of even more far-reaching effect. Reprinted in London in June, 1768, this two-shilling pamphlet quickly circulated through coffee-house and drawing-room. In ministerial circles the "Farmer" caused great indignation. In a letter from Franklin, addressed to his son, dated London, 13th of March, 1768, appears the following: "My Lord Hillsborough mentioned the 'Farmer's Letters' to me, said that he had read[xxvii] them, that they were well written, and he believed he could guess who was the author, looking in my face at the same time, as if he thought it was me. He censured the doctrines as extremely wild. I have read them as far as Number 8. I know not if any more have been published. I should, however, think they had been written by Mr. Delancey, not having heard any mention of the others you point out as joint authors."

Groaning under their own heavy taxation, the troubles of America had hitherto appealed but slightly to the average Englishman and the sympathies of the English people had become involved in the long-drawn-out struggles of Wilkes to obtain his constitutional rights. The press published little American news. America was little discussed; conditions there were practically unknown to all but the trading class, whose members had prospered through the monopoly of the constantly increasing commerce with the growing colonies. This class, naturally fearing the loss of the magnificent trade which had been built up, had long bemoaned the constantly increasing friction between the two factions on each side of the water. Englishmen in general had hitherto paid little attention to the debates over the various acts raising revenue from the colonies. From the time the "Farmer's Letters" were published in England[xxviii] the differences between Parliament and colonies were better understood there. Untouched and yet alarmed by the political corruption so prevalent at the time, thinking men saw in these "Letters" a warning that if their Sovereign was successful in his attempt to take away constitutional liberty from their fellow Englishmen across the sea, their own prized liberty at home was in danger. "American" news became more frequent in the newspapers, "Letters to the Printer," the form of editorials of the day, discussed and criticised the measures of Parliament with great freedom. To the masses, John Dickinson's name soon became very familiar through the agency of the press, which under date of June 26-28, 1768, freely noted Isaac Barré's characterization in the House of Commons of Dickinson as "a man who was not only an ornament to his country but an honor to human nature." Almost immediately after the publication of the London edition, the Monthly Review of July, 1768, forcibly called the attention of the literary world to the "Farmer's Letters" in an exhaustive review which is reprinted in the Notes, page liii, for the purpose of showing the view held by the English Whigs regarding the doctrines laid down and arguments used by Dickinson in defence of his position.

The "London Chronicle," under date of September 1st, 1768, printed the popular[xxix]Liberty song, written by Mr. Dickinson, and which, set to the inspiring air of "Hearts of Oak," was being sung throughout the colonies. In order to give the accompanying letter of request for the republication of the song, a request which, from its wording demonstrates the enthusiasm which the song aroused, the latter is here reprinted from the issue of the Boston "Evening Post" of August 22, 1768.

MESSIRS FLEETS

The following SONG being now much in Vogue and of late is heard resounding in almost all Companies in Town, and by way of eminence called "The Liberty Song," *you are desired to republish in your* 'circulating' Paper for the Benefit of the whole Continent of America.

[To the Tune of Hearts of Oak.]

Come, join Hand in Hand, brave Americans all,
And rouse your bold Hearts at fair *Liberty's* Call,
No *tyrannous Acts* shall suppress your *just Claim*,
Or stain with *dishonor* America's Name.

In Freedom we're *born*, & in Freedom we'll *live*,
Our Purses are ready,
Steady, Friends, Steady,
Not as *Slaves* but as *Freemen* our money we'll give.

Our worthy Forefathers—let's give them a Cheer—
To *Climates unknown* did courageously steer;
Thro' *Oceans* to *Deserts* for *Freedom* they came,
And dying bequeath'd us their *Freedom* & *Fame*.

In Freedom we're *born*, &c.

[xxx]

Their generous Bosoms all Dangers despis'd,
So *highly*, so *wisely*, their *Birthrights* they priz'd;
We'll keep what they gave—we will piously keep,
Nor frustrate their Toils on the Land or the Deep.

In Freedom we're *born*, &c.

The Tree their own Hands had to *Liberty* rear'd,
They liv'd to behold growing strong and rever'd;
With Transport then cry'd, 'now our Wishes we gain,
For our Children shall gather the Fruits of our Pain.'
    In Freedom we're *born*, &c.
    Swarms of *Placemen* and *Pensioners* soon will appear,
Like Locusts deforming the Charms of the Year;
Suns vainly will rise, Showers vainly descend,
If *we* are to *drudge for* what *others* shall *spend*.
    In Freedom we're *born*, &c.
    Then join Hand in Hand brave Americans all,
By *uniting* we stand, by *dividing* we fall;
In so righteous a Cause let us hope to succeed,
For Heaven approves of each generous Deed.
    In Freedom we're *born*, &c.
    All Ages shall speak with *amaze* and *applause*,
Of the *courage* we'll shew *in support of our laws*;
To die we can *bear*—but to serve we *disdain*—
For *Shame* is to *Freemen* more dreadful than *Pain*.
    In freedom we're *born*, &c.
    This Bumper I crown for our *Sovereign's* Health,
And this for *Britannia's* Glory and Wealth;
That Wealth and that Glory immortal may be,
If *She* is but *just*—and if *we* are but *free*.
[xxxi]
    In Freedom we're *born*, & in Freedom we'll *live*,
Our Purses are ready,
Steady, Friends, Steady,
Not as *Slaves*, but as *Freemen* our Money we'll give.

The following extract from the London "Chronicle" of October 4, 1768, demonstrates how completely the arguments and logic of the "Farmer's Letters" gained popular approval; how constantly Dickinson's name was kept before the public, both at home and abroad; how his fame was toasted; how he was recognized as the leader of political thought in the colonies. It shows also the constantly increasing interest in American matters taken by the press of England since the advent of the "Farmer's Letters," for the "American News," published in this and other London papers, was extensively reprinted in the local journals throughout the kingdom.

Taken from the Boston, in New England, Evening Post of August 22, 1768

On Monday the fifteenth instant, the anniversary of the ever memorable*Fourteenth of August*, was celebrated by the Sons of Liberty in this Town, with extraordinary festivity. At this Dawn, the British Flag was displayed on the *Tree of Liberty*, and a Discharge of *Fourteen* Cannon, ranged under the venerable Elm, saluted the joyous Day. At eleven o'clock, a very large Company of the principal Gentlemen and respectable Inhabitants of the Town, met at the Hall under the Tree,[xxxii] while the Streets were crowded with a Concourse of People of all Ranks, public Notice having been given of the intended Celebration. The Musick began at high Noon, performed on various Instruments, joined with Voices; and concluding with the universally admired *American* Song of Liberty,[4] the Grandeur of its Sentiment, and the easy Flow of its Numbers, together with an exquisite Harmony of Sound, afforded sublime Entertainment to a numerous Audience, fraught with a noble Ardour in the cause of Freedom: The Song was clos'd with the Discharge of Cannon and a Shout of Joy; at the same time the Windows of the Neighbouring Houses, were adorned with a brilliant appearance of the fair Daughters of Liberty, who testified their Approbation by Smiles of Satisfaction. The following Toasts succeeded, viz.

The following toasts may need brief explanation.—R. T. H. H.:

1. Our rightful Sovereign George the Third.

2. The Queen, Prince of Wales, and the rest of the Royal Family.

5

3. The Sons of Liberty throughout the World.

4. The glorious Administration of 1766.

4. The Rockingham Ministry which repealed the Stamp Act.

5. A perpetual Union of Great Britain and her Colonies, upon the immutable Principles of Justice and Equity.

6. May the sinister Designs of Oppressors, both in Great Britain and America, be for ever defeated.

7. May the common Rights of Mankind be established on the Ruin of all their Enemies.

[xxxiii]

8. Paschal Paoli and his brave Corsicans. May they never want the Support of the Friends of Liberty.

8. The struggles of Paoli and the Corsicans excited great interest both in Great Britain and America. Constant references are made to these in the "Letters."

9. The memorable 14th of August, 1765.

9. The day of the demonstration in Boston against the Stamp Officers. Daybreak disclosed hanging on a tree an effigy of the Stamp Officer Oliver. After hanging all day, at nightfall it was taken down by the Sons of Liberty, who placed it on a bier and escorted it through the principal streets in Boston to the home of Oliver, where, in the presence of a large number of people, it was burned.

10. *Magna Charta, and the Bill of Rights.*

11. *A speedy Repeal of unconstitutional Acts of Parliament, and a final Removal of illegal and oppressive Officers.*

12. The Farmer.

12. John Dickinson.

13. John Wilkes, *Esq.; and all independent Members of the British Parliament.*

14. The glorious Ninety-Two who defended the Rights of America, uninfluenced by the Mandates of a Minister, and undaunted by the threats of a Governor.

14. On the 11th day of February, 1768, the Assembly of Massachusetts adopted and sent to the various Colonial Assemblies a circular letter drawn up by Samuel Adams, informing them of the contents of a petition which the Massachusetts Assembly had sent to the King. This letter also urged united action against the oppressive measures of the Ministry, and gave great offense to the King and Ministry. The Secretary for the Colonies, Lord Hillsborough, instructed Governor Bernard of Massachusetts to order the Assembly to rescind this letter, and in case of refusal to dissolve this body. After a thorough discussion this request was refused by a vote of "ninety-two" to "seventeen."

Which being finished, the French horns sounded; and after another discharge of the cannon, compleating the number Ninety-Two, the[xxxiv]gentlemen in their carriages repaired to the Greyhound Tavern in Roxbury, where a *frugal* and *elegant* entertainment was provided. The music played during the repast: After which the following toasts were given out, and the repeated discharge of cannon spoke the general assent.

1. The King.

2. Queen and Royal Family.

3. Lord Cambden.

3. A strenuous upholder of the Constitutional rights of the Colonies and a strong defender in the House of Lords of the doctrine, "No taxation without representation." Contemporary writers frequently spelt Camden's name as above.

4. Lord Chatham.

5. Duke of Richmond.

5. Another friend of America in the same body.

6. Marquis of Rockingham.

6. Under whose ministry the Stamp Act was repealed.

7. General Conway.

7. The leader in the House of Commons during the Rockingham Ministry.

8. Lord Dartmouth.

8. President of the Board of Trade in the Rockingham Ministry, much loved in the Colonies. Dartmouth College bears his name.

9. Earl of Chesterfield.

9. A warm adherent of America.

10. Colonel Barre.

10. The companion of Wolfe at Quebec; in replying to Townsend during one of the debates over the passage of the Stamp Acts he characterized the Americans as "Sons of Liberty," a term which immediately was applied throughout the Colonies to those who were resenting the interference of Parliament with their home government.

11. General Howard.

11. A member of Parliament from Stamford who was active in [xxxv]obtaining the repeal of the Stamp Act.

12. Sir George Saville.

12. Represented Yorkshire in the House of Commons; a strong supporter of the Rockingham Ministry.

13. Sir William Meredith.

13. Member of Parliament from Liverpool. Lord of the Admiralty

14. Sir William Baker.

14. Also energetic in securing the repeal of the Stamp Act.

15. John Wilkes, *Esq., and a Speedy Reversal of his outlawry.*

15. The struggles of Wilkes excited keen interest in America.

16. The Farmer of Pennsylvania.

16. It is noted that this was the second time Dickinson's health was drunk that day. No other American residing in this country was toasted.

17. The Massachusetts Ninety-Two.

18. Prosperity and Perpetuity to the British Empire, *on Constitutional Principles.*

19. North America: *And her fair Daughters of Liberty.*

20. The illustrious Patriots of the Kingdom of Ireland.

20. In Letter X Dickinson warns against the fate of Ireland.

21. The truly heroic Paschal Paoli, *and all the brave Corsicans.*

22. The downfall of arbitrary and despotic Power *in all Parts of the Earth; and Liberty without* Licentiousness *to all mankind.*

23. A perpetual Union and Harmony between Great Britain *and the Colonies, on the Principles of the Original Compact.*

24. To the immortal Memory of that Hero of Heroes *William the Third.*

25. The speedy Establishment of a wise and permanent [xxxvi]administration.

26. The right *noble Lords, and* very worthy *Commoners, who voted for the Repeal of the* stamp Act *from* Principle.

27. Dennis De Berdt, *Esq; and all the true Friends of* America *in Great Britain, and those of Great Britain in America.*

27. The agent of Massachusetts in London.

28. The respectable *Towns of* Salem, Ipswich and Marblehead, *with all the Absentees from the late Assembly, and their* constituents, *who have publickly approved of the Vote against* Rescinding.

28. Representatives of these towns voted in favor of rescinding. Town meetings, however, were held, and the citizens of these places recorded themselves as endorsing the action of the majority in refusing the "Ministerial Mandates" and condemned the position assumed by their own representatives. In letters which appeared in the press a number of absentees from the Assembly boldly endorsed the action of the majority.

29. May all Patriots *be as wise as Serpents, and as harmless as Doves.*

30. The Manufactories *of* North America, *and the* Banishment *of Luxury,* Dissipation and *other Vices, Foreign and Domestic.*

30. Referring to the proposal of Dickinson quoted on page xxiii of the Introduction.

31. The removal of all Task-Masters, and an effectual Redress of all other Grievances.

32. The Militia *of* Great Britain *and of the* Colonies.

33. As Iron sharpeneth Iron, *so may the Countenance of every good and virtuous Son and Daughter of Liberty, that of his or her* [xxxvii]*Friend.*

34. The Assemblies on this vast and rapidly populating Continent, who have treated a late haughty and "merely ministerial" Mandate "with all that Contempt it so justly deserves."

34. Referring to the replies of the various Assemblies to the circular letter and endorsements of the action of the Massachusetts Assembly.

35. Strong Halters and sharp axes to all such as respectively deserve them.

36. Scalping   Savages let   loose   in Tribes, rather   than Legions   of   Placemen, Pensioners, and Walkerizing Dragoons.

37. The Amputation of any Limb, if it be necessary to preserve the Body Politic from Perdition.

38. The oppressed and distressed foreign Protestants.

39. The free and independent Cantons of Switzerland.

40. Their High Mightinesses the States General of Seven United Provinces.

41. The King of Prussia.

42. The Republic of Letters.

43. The Liberty of the Press.

44. Spartan, Roman, British Virtue, and Christian Graces joined.

45. Every man under his own Vine! under his own Fig-Tree! None to make us afraid! And let all the People say, Amen!

45. See page 51.

Upon this happy occasion, the whole company with the approbation of their brethren in Roxbury, consecrated a tree in the vicinity; under the shade [xxxviii]of which, on some future anniversary, they say they shall commemorate the day, which shall liberate America from her present oppression! Then making an agreeable excursion round Jamaica Pond, in which excursion they received the kind salutation of a Friend to the cause by the discharge of cannon at six o'clock they returned to Town; and passing in slow and orderly procession through the principal streets, and the State-House, they retired to their respective dwellings. It is allowed that this cavalcade surpassed all that has ever been seen in America. The joy of the day was manly, and an uninterrupted regularity presided through the whole.

The two illustrations in this volume were selected for the purpose of recording prevalent contemporary opinions of Dickinson.

The frontispiece is a reproduction (slightly reduced in size)[5] of the very scarce print in which John Dickinson is crudely portrayed as the author of the "Farmer's Letters." It was first advertised for sale in the Pennsylvania "Chronicle" under date of October 12-17, 1768, as follows:

Lately published and sold by R. Bell
at JAMES EMERSON'S, in Market-street,
near the river, and at JOHN
HART'S vendue store, in Southward
(Price One Shilling)
an elegant engraved COPPER PLATE PRINT
of the PATRIOTIC AMERICAN FARMER;
The same glazed and framed, price Five Shillings.

[xxxix]

This specimen of early American engraving, the work of some unknown artist and engraver, was undoubtedly inspired by the following article which appeared in the Pennsylvania "Chronicle" for May, 9-16, 1768, as well as the many other newspapers in the colonies, so eager was the press to publish any information concerning the author of the "Farmer's Letters." The inscription is thus explained as well as the elimination of the vowels from Dickinson's name.

PHILADELPHIA

On Tuesday last, by order of the Governor and Society of Fort St. David's, fourteen Gentlemen, members of that Company, waited upon J-n D-ck-nson Esq; and presented the following address, in a Box of Heart of Oak.

RESPECTED SIR,

When a Man of Abilities, prompted by Love of his Country, exerts them in her Cause, and renders her the most eminent Services, *not to be sensible,* of the Benefits received, is Stupidity; *not to be grateful for them,* is Baseness.

Influenced by this Sentiment, we, the Governor and Company of Fort St. David's, who among other Inhabitants of *British America,* are indebted to you for your most excellent

and generous Vindication of Liberties dearer to us than our Lives, beg Leave to return you our heartiest Thanks, and offer to you the greatest Mark of Esteem, that, as a Body, it is in our Power to bestow, by admitting you, as we hereby do, a Member of our Society.

[xl]

When that destructive Project of *Taxation*, which your Integrity and Knowledge so signally contributed to baffle about two years ago, was lately renewed under a *Disguise* so *artfully contrived* as to delude Millions, You, sir, *watchful* for the Interests of Your Country, *perfectly* acquainted with them, and *undaunted* in asserting them, ALONE detected the Monster concealed from others by an altered Appearance, exposed it, stripped of its insidious covering, in its own horrid Shape, and, we firmly trust by the Blessing of God on Your Wisdom and Virtue, will again extricate the *British* Colonies on this Continent from the cruel Snares of Oppression; for we already perceive these Colonies ROUSED *by your strong and seasonable* Call, pursuing the salutary Measures advised by You for obtaining Redress.

Nor is this all that you have performed for Your NATIVE LAND. *Animated by a sacred* Zeal, *guided by Truth and supported by Justice,* YOU *have penetrated to the Foundations of the Constitution,* have *poured* the clearest Light on the important *Points,* hitherto involved in a Darkness bewildering even the Learned, and have *established* with an amazing Force and Plainness of Argument, the TRUE DISTINCTIONS and GRAND PRINCIPLES, that will *fully instruct Ages* YET UNBORN, what Rights belong to them, and the best Methods of defending them.

To Merit far less distinguished, ancient *Greece* or *Rome* would have decreed Statues and Honours without Number: But it is *Your Fortune* and *your Glory,* Sir, that You live in *such* Times, and possess *such exalted Worth,* that the *Envy* of those, whose *Duty* it is to applaud You, can conceive no other Consolation, than by withholding those Praises in Public, which all honest Men acknowledge in Private that you have deserved.

We present to you, sir, a small gift of a Society not dignified by any legal authority; But when you consider this gift as expressive of the *sincere Affection* of many of your Fellow Citizens for Your Person, and of their *unlimited Approbation* of the noble Principles maintained in your unequalled[xli] Labours, we hope this Testimony of our Sentiments will be acceptable to you.

May that all-gracious Being, which in kindness to these colonies gave your valuable Life Existence *at the critical Period* when it will be most wanted, grant it a long Continuance, filled with every Felicity; and when your Country sustains its dreadful loss, may you enjoy the Happiness of Heaven, and on Earth may your Memory be cherished, as we doubt not it will be, to the latest Posterity.

Signed by the Order of the Society,

JOHN BAYARD, Secretary.

The box was finely decorated, and the Inscription neatly done in Letters of Gold. On the Top was represented the Cap of Liberty on a Spear, resting on a Cypher of the Letters I. D. Underneath the Cypher in a semicircular Label——Pro Patria——Around the whole the following words:

THE GIFT OF THE GOVERNOR AND SOCIETY OF FORT ST. DAVID'S TO THE AUTHOR OF THE FARMER'S LETTERS, IN GRATEFUL TESTIMONY OF THE VERY EMINENT SERVICES THEREBY RENDERED TO THIS COUNTRY, 1768.

On the Inside of the Top—

THE LIBERTIES OF
THE BRITISH COLONIES IN AMERICA
ASSERTED
WITH ATTIC ELOQUENCE,
AND ROMAN SPIRIT,
BY
J-N D-K-NS-N[ol] ESQR.;
BARRISTER AT LAW.

On the Inside of the Bottom—

ITA CUIQUE EVENIAT
UT DE REPUBLICA MERUIT.

On the Outside of the Bottom—A sketch of *Fort St. David's.*
[xlii]

To which the following Answer was returned.

GENTLEMEN,

I very gratefully receive the Favour you have been pleased to bestow upon me, in admitting me a Member of your Company; and I return you my heartiest Thanks for your Kindness.

The "Esteem" of worthy Fellow Citizens is a Treasure of greatest Price; and as no man can more highly value it than I do, Your Society in "expressing the Affection" of so many respectable Persons for me, affords Me the sincerest Pleasure.

Nor will this Pleasure be lessened by reflecting, that you may have regarded with a generous *Partiality* my Attempts to promote the Welfare of our Country; for the Warmth of your Praises in commending a Conduct you*suppose* to deserve them, gives Worth to these Praises, by proving *your*Merit, while you attribute Merit to *another*.

Your Characters, gentlemen, did not need this Evidence to convince Me, how much I ought to prize Your "Esteem" or how much You deserved*Mine.*

I think myself extremely fortunate, in having obtained your favorable Opinion, which I shall constantly and carefully endeavor to preserve.

I most heartily wish you every Kind of Happiness, and particularly that you may enjoy the comfortable Prospect of transmitting to your Posterity those "Liberties" dearer to You than your Lives, "which God gave to you, and which no *inferior Power* has a Right to take away."

CHELSEA DERBY PORCELAIN STATUETTE OF CATHERINE MACAULAY

The potter's art, which from time immemorial has been the means of transmitting history, furnishes the other illustration and also perpetuates the estimate of Dickinson's character held by William Duesbury, England's greatest manufacturer of porcelain. It pictures a porcelain statuette of Mrs. Catherine[xliii]
[xliv]
[xlv] Macaulay, a well-known historian, whose "History of England from the Accession of James the First to that of the Brunswick Line" and other historical writings met with great approval among the Whig party in England and whose decided approval of the stand taken by the colonies, gave her great popularity in America. This statuette, measuring 13½ inches in height, is modeled to a certain extent after the statue of this lady which was erected in 1777 in the Church of St. Stephen, Walbrook, London. Mrs. Macaulay appears leaning upon her "Histories of England," which rest on the top of a pedestal, on the front of which is the inscription, "Government a Power Delegated for the Happiness of Mankind conducted by Wisdom, Justice and Mercy." Beneath are the words, "*American Congress.*" On the side of the pedestal the name of *Dickinson* appears, preceded by the names of those noble writers, England's great advocates and expounders of Constitutional liberty, Sydney, Hampden, Milton, Locke, Harrington, Ludlow and Marvel. This beautiful porcelain statuette was moulded at the Chelsea factory in 1777, the same year in which Boswell chronicles Dr. Johnson's visit there, noting, "The china was beautiful, but Dr. Johnson justly observed it was too dear, for he could have vessels of silver as cheap as were here made of porcelain."

The space at my disposal prevents my[xlvi] quoting many a "Letter to the Printer" appealing for justice for the Colonials as well as numerous contributed articles which appeared during the next few years in the English press, the contents of which clearly show how strongly Dickinson's arguments had influenced their respective authors. While it is true that these sentiments were attacked both at home and abroad, the attacks soon lost their vehemence. Strange as it may seem, more protests against the course of the ministry than denunciations of the doings of the colonial Assemblies are found in the columns of the English press of the period. The demand for the arguments contained in the "Farmer's Letters" was not lessened by subsequent events as their popularity demanded the publishing of another London edition in 1774.

Certainly to John Dickinson for his masterly defence of the rights of the Colonies America owes an everlasting debt of gratitude. The logic of his claims and his warnings as to what must be the ultimate result of the ministerial encroachments upon the liberties of Englishmen did much to win over to the American cause in England that strong ally, the support of a large body of thoughtful Englishmen. These men actively condemned the ministerial actions and during the war which followed caused the course of the government to be bitterly opposed by an influential and constantly[xlvii] growing minority in Parliament. Through their efforts was fostered a public sentiment which caused the war to be prosecuted in a half-hearted manner and obliged a power-loving King to fill the depleted ranks of his army with German mercenaries, so impossible was it to force a sufficient number of his own liberty-loving subjects to fight against their kindred living in the land so happily alluded to by a contributor to the London "Chronicle" (June 3-6, 1769), in the following poem:

The Genius of America *to her Sons*

Who'd know the sweets of Liberty?
'Tis to climbe the mountain's brow,
Thence to discern rough industry,
At the harrow or the plough;
'Tis where my sons their crops have sown,
Calling the harvest all their own;
'Tis where the heart to truth allied,
Never felt unmanly fear;
'Tis where the eye with milder pride,
Nobly sheds sweet pity's tear;
Such as America yet shall see,
These are the sweets of Liberty.

[xlviii]
[xlix]
[l]
[li]

NOTES.
I.

An address from the Moderator and Freemen of the Town of Providence in the Colony of Rhode-Island, and Providence Plantation convened in open Meeting the 20th day of June, 1768, to the Author of a Series of Letters signed

A FARMER.

Sir,

In your Retirement, "near the Banks of the River Delaware," where you are compleating, in a rational way, the Number of Days allotted to you by Divine Goodness, the consciousness of having employed those Talents which God hath bestowed upon You, for the Support of our Rights, must afford you a Satisfaction vastly exceeding that, which is derived to you from the universal Approbation of Your Letters,—However amidst the general Acclamation of your Praise, we the Moderator and Freemen of the ancient Town of Providence cannot be silent; although we would not offend your Delicacy, or incur the Imputation of Flattery in expressing our Gratitude to you.

Your Benevolence to Mankind, fully discoverable from your Writings, doubtless caused you to address your countrymen, whom you tenderly call *Dear* and *Beloved,* in a Series of Letters, wherein you have with a great Judgment, and in the most spirited and forcible Manner explained their Rights and Privileges; and vindicated them against such as would reduce these extensive Dominions[lii] of His Majesty to Poverty, Misery, and Slavery. This Your patriotic Exertion in our Cause and indeed in the Cause of all the human Race in some Degree, hath rendered you very dear to us, although we know not your Person.

We deplore the Frailty of human Nature, in that it is necessary that we should be frequently awakened into Attention to our Duty in Matters very plain and incontrovertible, if we would suffer ourselves to consider them. From this Inattention to Things evidently the

Duty and Interest of the World, we suppose despotic Rule to have originated, and all the Train of Miseries consequent thereupon.

The virtuous and good Man, who rouses an injured Country from their Lethargy, and animates them into active and successful Endeavours for casting off the Burdens imposed on them, and effecting a full Enjoyment of the Rights of Men, which no Human Creature ought to violate, will merit the warmest Expressions of Gratitude from his Countrymen, for his Instrumentality in saving them and their Posterity.

As the very Design of instituting civil Government in the World was to secure to Individuals a quiet Enjoyment of their native Rights, wherever there is a Departure from this great and only End, impious Force succeeds. The Blessings of a just Government, and the Horror of brutal Violence are both inexpressible. As the latter is generally brought upon People by Degrees, it will be their Duty to watch against even the smallest attempt to "innovate a single Iota" in their Privilege.

With Hearts truly loyal to the King, we feel the greatest concern at divers Acts of the British Parliament, relative to these colonies. We are clear and unanimous in Sentiment that they are[liii] subversive of our Liberties, and derogatory to the Power and Dignity of the several Legislatures established in America.

Permit us, Sir, to assure you that we feel an ineffable Gratitude to you, for sending forth your Letters at a Time when the Exercise of great Abilities was necessary. We sincerely wish that You may see the Fruit of your Labours. We on our parts shall be ready at all Times to evince to the World that we will not surrender our privileges to any of our Fellow Subjects, but will earnestly contend for them, hoping that the "Almighty will look upon our righteous contest with gracious approbation." We hope that the Conduct of the Colonies on this Occasion will be "peaceable, prudent, firm, and joint; and such as will show their Loyalty to the best of Sovereigns, and that they know what they owe to themselves as well as to Great-Britain."

Signed by Order

JAMES ANGELL, Town Clerk.

II.
FROM THE MONTHLY REVIEW. LONDON, JULY, 1768.

"Letters from a Farmer in Pennsylvania, to the Inhabitants of the British Colonies. 8vo. 2s. Almon. 1768.

"We have, in the Letters now before us, a calm yet full inquiry into the right of the British parliament, lately assumed, to tax the American colonies; the unconstitutional nature of which attempt is maintained in a well-connected chain of close and manly reasoning; and though from this character, it is evident that detached passages[liv] must appear to a disadvantage, yet it is but just to give our Readers some specimens of the manner in which the author asserts the rights of his American brethren; subjects of the British government, as he pleads, carrying their birthrights with them wherever they settle as such.

'Colonies, says he, were formerly planted by warlike nations, to keep their enemies in awe; to relieve their country overburthened with inhabitants; or to discharge a number of discontented and troublesome citizens. But in more modern ages, the spirit of violence being, in some measure, if the expression may be allowed, sheathed in commerce, colonies have been settled by the nations of Europe for the purposes of trade. These purposes were to be attained, by the colonies raising for their mother country those things which she did not produce herself; and by supplying themselves from her with things they wanted. These were the *national* objects in the commencement of our colonies, and have been uniformly so in their promotion.

'To answer these grand purposes, perfect liberty was known to be necessary; all history proving, that trade and freedom are nearly related to each other. By a due regard to this wise and just plan, the infant colonies, exposed in the unknown climates and unexplored wildernesses of this new world, lived, grew, and flourished.

'The parent country, with undeviating prudence and virtue, attentive to the first principles of colonization, drew to herself the benefits she might reasonably expect, and preserved to her children the blessings, upon which those benefits were founded. She made laws, obliging her colonies to carry to her all those products which she wanted for her own use; and all those raw materials which she chose herself to work up. Besides this restriction, she forbade them to procure *manufactures* from any other part of the globe, or even the *products* of *European* countries, which alone could rival her,[lv]without being first brought to her. In short, by a variety of laws, she regulated their trade in such a manner as she thought most conducive to their mutual advantage and her own welfare. A power was reserved to the crown of *repealing* any laws that should be enacted: the executive authority of government was also lodged in the crown, and its representatives; and an*appeal* was secured to the crown from all judgments in the administration of justice.

'For all these powers, established by the mother country over the colonies; for all these immense emoluments derived by her from them; for all their difficulties and distresses in fixing themselves, what was the recompense made them? A communication of her rights in general, and particularly of that great one, the foundation of all the rest—that their property, acquired with so much pain and hazard, should be disposed of by none but themselves—or, to use beautiful and emphatic language of the sacred scriptures, "that they should sit *every man* under his vine, and under his fig-tree, and *none should make them afraid*."

'Can any man of candour and knowledge deny that these institutions form an affinity between Great Britain and her colonies, that sufficiently secures their dependence upon her? Or that for her to levy taxes upon them is to reverse the nature of things? Or that she can pursue such a measure without reducing them to a state of vassalage?

'If any person cannot conceive the supremacy of Great Britain to exist, without the power of laying taxes to levy money upon us, the history of the colonies, and of Great Britain, since their settlement, will prove the contrary. He will there find the amazing advantages arising to her from them—the constant exercise of her supremacy—and their filial submission to it, without a single rebellion, or even the thought of one, from their first emigration to this moment—and all these things have happened, without one instance of[lvi] Great Britain's laying taxes to levy money upon them.

'How many British authors have demonstrated, that the present wealth, power and glory of their country, are founded upon these colonies? As constantly as streams tend to the ocean have they been pouring the fruits of all their labours into their mother's lap. Good heaven! and shall a total oblivion of former tendernesses and blessings, be spread over the minds of a good and wise nation by the sordid arts of intriguing men, who, covering their selfish projects under pretences of public good, first enrage their countrymen into a frenzy of passion, and then advance their own influence and interest, by gratifying the passion, which they themselves have basely excited.

'Hitherto Great Britain has been contented with her prosperity, moderation has been the rule of her conduct. But now, a generous, humane people, that so often have protected the liberty of *strangers*, is inflamed into an attempt to tear a privilege from her own children, which if executed, must, in their opinion, sink them into slaves: *and for what?* for a pernicious power, not necessary to her as her own experience may convince her; but horribly dreadful and detestable to her.

'It seems extremely probable, that when cool, dispassionate prosperity, shall consider the affectionate intercourse, the reciprocal benefits, and the unsuspecting confidence, that have subsisted between these colonies and their parent country, for such a length of time, they will execrate, with the bitterest curses, the infamous memory of those men, whose pestilential ambition unnecessarily, wantonly, first opened the sources of civil discord between them; first turned their love into jealousy; and first taught these provinces, filled with grief and anxiety, to enquire.'

"As every community possessed of valuable privileges, and desirous to preserve the enjoyment of them, ought to be very cautious of admitting[lvii] innovations from their established forms of political administration, our Author does not confine his views to the immediate effects of the laws lately passed regarding America; but considers the necessary tendency of the precedents; thus he says,

'I have looked over every *statute* relating to these colonies, from their first settlement to this time; and I find everyone of them founded on this principle, till the *stamp-act* administration. *All before*, are calculated to regulate trade, and preserve or promote a mutually beneficial intercourse between the several constituent parts of the empire; and though many of them imposed duties on trade, yet those duties were always imposed *with design* to restrain the commerce of one part, that was injurious to another, and thus to promote the general welfare. The raising a revenue thereby was never intended. Thus, the king by his judges in his courts of justice, impose fines, which altogether amount to a very considerable sum, and contribute to the support of government; but this is merely a consequence arising from restrictions, that only meant to keep peace, and prevent confusion; and surely a man would argue very loosely, who should conclude from hence, that the king has a right to levy money in general upon his subjects. Never did the British parliament, till the period above mentioned, think of imposing duties in America, *for the purpose of raising a revenue.* Mr. Grenville first introduced this language, in the preamble to the fourth of George III. chap. 15, which has these words—"and whereas it is just and necessary that *a revenue be raised in your majesty's said dominions in America, for defraying the expenses of defending, protecting and securing the same.* We your majesty's most dutiful and loyal subjects, *the commons of Great Britain,* in Parliament assembled, being desirous to make some provisions in this present session of parliament, *towards raising the said revenue in America,* have resolved to *give* and *grant* unto your majesty the several rates and duties hereinafter mentioned," etc.

[lviii]

'A few months after came the *stamp-act,* which reciting this, proceeds in the same strange mode of expression, thus—"And whereas it is just and necessary, that provision be made *for raising a further revenue within your majesty's dominions in America, towards defraying the said expenses,* we your majesty's most dutiful and loyal subjects, the *commons* of *Great Britain, etc., give and grant,*" etc., as before.

'The last act, granting duties upon paper, etc., carefully pursues these modern precedents. The preamble is, "Whereas it is expedient, *that a revenue should be raised in your majesty's dominions in America for making a more certain and adequate provision for defraying the charge of the administration of justice, and the support of civil government in such provinces, where it shall be found necessary; and towards the further defraying of the expences of defending, protecting, and securing the said dominions,* we your majesty's most dutiful and loyal subjects, the *commons* of *Great Britain,* etc. give *and grant,*" etc. as before.

'Here we may observe an authority expresly claimed and exerted to impose duties on these colonies; not for the regulation of trade; not for the preservation or promotion of a mutually beneficial intercourse between the several constituent parts of the empire, heretofore the *sole objects* of parliamentary institutions; *but for the single purpose of levying money upon us.*'

"Again in another place,

'What but the indisputable, the acknowledged exclusive right of the colonies to tax themselves, could be the reason, that in this long period of more than one hundred and fifty years, no statute was ever passed for the sole purpose of raising a revenue from the colonies? And how clear, how cogent must that reason be, to which every parliament, and every ministry for so long a time submitted, without a single attempt to innovate?

'England, in part of that course of years, and[lix] Great Britain, in other parts, was engaged in several fierce and expensive wars; troubled with some tumultuous and bold parliaments; governed by many daring and wicked ministers; yet none of them ever ventured to touch the Palladium of American liberty. Ambition, avarice, faction, tyranny, all revered it. Whenever it was necessary to raise money on the colonies, the requisitions of the crown were made, and dutifully complied with. The parliament, from time to time, regulated their trade, and that of the rest of the empire, to preserve their dependence and the connections of the whole in good order.'

"The amount of present duties exacted in an unusual way is no part of the object in question; for our Pennsylvanian Farmer observes:

'Some persons may think this act of no consequence, because the duties are so *small.* A fatal error. *That* is the very circumstance most alarming to me. For I am convinced, that the authors of this law would never have obtained an act to raise so trifling a sum as it must do, had they not intended by it to establish a *precedent* for future use. To console ourselves with the *smallness* of the duties, is to walk deliberately into the snare that is set for us, praising the *neatness* of the workmanship. Suppose the duties imposed by the late act could be paid by

14

these distressed colonies with the utmost ease, and that the purposes to which they are to be applied, were the most reasonable and equitable that can be conceived, the contrary of which I hope to demonstrate before these letters are concluded; yet even in such a supposed case, these colonies ought to regard the act with abhorrence. For who are a free people? Not those, over whom government is reasonably and equitably exercised, but those, who live under a government so *constitutionally checked* and controuled, that proper provision is made against its being otherwise exercised.

[lx]

'The late act is founded on the destruction of this constitutional security. If the parliament have a right to lay a duty of four shillings and eight pence on a hundred weight of glass, or a ream of paper, they have a right to lay a duty of any other sum on either. They may raise the duty, as the author before quoted says has been done in some countries, till it "exceeds seventeen or eighteen times the value of the commodity." In short, if they have a right to levy a tax of *one penny* upon us, they have a right to levy a *million* upon us; for where does their right stop? At any given number of pence, shillings or pounds? To attempt to limit their right, after granting it to exist at all, is as contrary to reason—as granting it to exist at all, is contrary to justice. If they have any right to tax us—then, whether our own money shall continue in our pockets or not, depends no longer on *us*, but on *them*, "There is nothing which "we" can call our own; or, to use the words of Mr. Locke—*what property have "we" in that which another may, by right, take, when he pleases, to himself?*"

'These duties which will inevitably be levied upon us—which are now levying upon us—are *expresly laid for the sole purpose of taking money*. This is the true definition of "taxes." They are therefore *taxes*. This money is to be taken from *us*. We are therefore *taxed. Those* who are *taxed* without their own consent, expressed by themselves or their representatives are *slaves. We are taxed* without our own consent, expressed by ourselves or representatives. *We* are therefore slaves.'

"Further,

'Indeed nations in general are more apt to *feel* than to *think*; and therefore nations in general have lost their liberty: for as the violation of the rights of the governed are commonly not only *specious*, but *small* at the beginning, they spread over the multitude in such a manner, as to touch individuals but slightly; thus they are disregarded. The[lxi] power or profit that arises from these violations, *centering in a few persons*, is to them considerable. For this reason, the *Governors* having in view their particular purposes, successively preserve an uniformity of conduct for attaining them: they regularly increase and multiply the first injuries, till at length the inattentive people are compelled to perceive the heaviness of their burthen. They begin to complain and inquire—but too late. They find their oppressions so strengthened by success, and themselves so entangled in examples of express authority on the part of their rulers, and of tacit recognition on their own part, that they are quite confounded: for millions entertain no other idea of the *legality* of power, than that it is founded on the exercise of power. They then voluntarily fasten their chains by adopting a pusillanimous opinion "that there will be too much danger in attempting a remedy"—or another opinion no less fatal, "that the government has a *right* to treat them as it does." They then seek a wretched relief for their minds, by persuading themselves, that to yield their *obedience*, is to discharge their *duty*. The *deplorable* poverty of spirit, that prostrates all the dignity bestowed by Divine Providence on our nature—of course succeeds.'

"With regard to the proper conduct of the colonies on this occasion he premises the following questions:

'Has not the parliament *expressly avowed* their *intention* of raising money from us for *certain* purposes? Is not this scheme *popular* in Great Britain? Will the taxes imposed by the late act, *answer* those purposes? If it will, must it not take an immense sum from us? If it will not, is it to be *expected*, that the parliament will not *fully execute* their *intention*, when it is pleasing at home, *and not opposed* here? Must not this be done by imposing *new taxes*? Will not every addition thus made to our taxes, be an addition to the power of the British legislature, *by increasing the number of officers* employed in the collection?[lxii] Will not every additional tax therefore render it *more difficult* to abrogate any of them? When a branch of revenue is once established, does it not appear to many people *invidious* and undutiful, to attempt to abolish it? If taxes sufficient to *accomplish* the intention of the parliament, are imposed by the parliament, what taxes will remain to be imposed by our assemblies? If *no material* taxes remain to be imposed by them, what must become of *them*, and the people they represent?'

"Our Author all along, however, asserts that the real interest of English America consists in its proper dependence on the mother country, at the same time that he strenuously exhorts his countrymen to oppose, by all the suitable means in their power, every incroachment on those constitutions under the sanction of which they settled on those remote and uncultivated shores, whereon they have so industriously established themselves. He remarks with a spirit which no one, it is apprehended, can condemn:

'I am no further concerned in anything affecting America, than any one of you; and when liberty leaves it, I can quit it much more conveniently than most of you: but while divine providence, that gave me existence in a land of freedom, permits my head to think, my lips to speak, and my hands to move, I shall so highly and gratefully value the blessing received, as to take care, that my silence and inactivity shall not give my implied assent to any act, degrading my brethren and myself from the birthright, wherewith heaven itself "hath made us free.'

"The consequence of Great Britain exerting this disagreeable power, he shews, in a long train of arguments, to have a tendency very fatal to the liberty of America, which he illustrates by examining into the application of the pensions on the[lxiii] Irish establishment; and sums up his reasoning with the following positions:

'Let these *truths* be indelibly impressed on our mind—*that we cannot be* happy, *without being* free—that we cannot be free, *without being secure*—in our property—that we cannot be secure in our property, if, *without our consent, others may, as by right, take it away*—that *taxes imposed on us by parliament*, do thus take it away—that *duties laid for the sole purposes of raising money*, are taxes—that attempts to lay such duties *should be instantly and firmly opposed*—that this opposition can never be effectual, unless it is the united effort of those provinces—that therefore *benevolence of temper towards each other*, and *unanimity of counsels*, are essential to the welfare of the whole—and lastly, that for this reason, every man amongst us, who in any manner would encourage either dissention, diffidence, or indifference, between these colonies, is an enemy to *himself*, and to *his country*.

'The belief of these truths, I verily think, my countrymen, is indispensably necessary to your happiness. I beseech you, therefore, "teach them diligently unto your children, and talk of them when you sit in your houses, and when you walk by the way, and when you lie down and when you rise up."

'*What* have these colonies to *ask*, while they continue free? or what have they to *dread*, but insidious attempts to subvert their freedom? *Their prosperity* does not depend on *ministerial favours doled* out to particular provinces. *They* form one political body, of which *each* colony is a *member*. *Their happiness* is founded on their constitution; and is to be promoted by preserving that constitution in unabated vigour, *throughout every part*. A spot, a speck of decay, however small the limb on which it appears, and however remote it may seem from the vitals, should be alarming. We have *all the rights* requisite for our prosperity. The *legal authority* of Great Britain may indeed lay hard restrictions[lxiv] upon us; but, like the spear of Telephus, it will cure as well as wound. Her unkindness will instruct and compel us, after some time to discover, in our *industry* and *frugality*, surprising remedies—*if our rights continue* unviolated: for as long as the *products* of our *labour*, and the *rewards* of our *care*, can properly be called *our own*, so long will it be worth our while to be *industrious* and *frugal*. But if we plow—sow—reap—gather and thresh—we find, that we plow—sow—reap—gather and thresh *for others*, whose pleasure is to be the SOLE limitation *how much* they shall *take* and *how much* they *shall leave*, WHY should we repeat the unprofitable toil? Horses and oxen are content with *that portion of the fruits of their work*, which their *owners* assign to them, in order to keep them strong enough to raise successive crops; but even *these beasts* will not submit to draw for their masters, until they are *subdued* with *whips* and *goads*. Let us take care of our rights, and we *therein* take care of our *property*. "SLAVERY IS EVER PRECEDED BY SLEEP." *Individuals* may be *dependent* on ministers if they please. *States should scorn it*; and if *you* are not wanting to yourselves, you will have a *proper regard* paid *you* by *those*, to whom if you are not *respectable*, you will infallibly be contemptible. But—*if we have already forgot* the *reasons* that urged us, with unexampled unanimity, to exert ourselves two years ago—if *our zeal* for the *public good* is *worn out* before the *homespun cloaths* which it caused us to have made—if *our* resolutions are so faint, as by our present conduct to *condemn* our own late *successful* example—if *we are not affected* by any reverence for the memory of our ancestors, who transmitted to us that freedom in which they had been blest—if *we are not animated* by any regard for posterity, to whom, by the most sacred obligations, we are bound to deliver down the invaluable inheritance—THEN, indeed, any *minister,* or any *tool* of a minister, or any *creature* of a tool of a minister—or any *lower instrument* of *administration,* if lower there be, is a *personage* whom it may be dangerous to offend.'

[lxv]

"In justification of the Letter-writer's loyalty, and the integrity of his intentions, he declares in a note:

'If any person shall imagine that he discovers in these letters the least disaffection towards our most excellent sovereign, and the parliament of Great Britain, or the least dislike of the dependence of these colonies on that kingdom, I beg that such person will not form any judgment on *particular expressions,* but will consider the *tenour* of all the letters taken together. In that case, I flatter myself that every unprejudiced reader will be *convinced,* that the true interests of Great Britain are as dear to me as they ought to be to every good subject.

'If I am an enthusiast in anything, it is in my zeal for the *perpetual dependance* of these colonies on the mother country.—A dependance founded on mutual benefits, the continuance of which can be secured only by *mutual affections.* Therefore it is, that with extreme apprehension I view the smallest seeds of discontent, which are unwarily scattered abroad. Fifty or sixty years will make astonishing alterations in these colonies; and this consideration should render it the business of Great Britain more and more to cultivate our good dispositions toward her: but the misfortune is, that those *great men,* who are wrestling for power at home, think themselves very slightly interested in the prosperity of their country *fifty* or *sixty* years hence; but are deeply concerned in blowing up a popular clamour for supposed *immediate advantages.*

'For my part, I regard Great Britain as a *bulwark* happily fixed between these colonies and the powerful nations of Europe. That kingdom is our advanced post or fortification, *which remaining safe,* we under its protection enjoying peace, may diffuse the blessings of religion, science, and liberty, through remote wildernesses. It is, therefore, incontestably our *duty* and our *interest* to support the strength of Great Britain. When, confiding [lxvi] in that strength, she begins to forget from whence it arose, it will be an easy thing to shew the source. She may readily be reminded of the loud alarm spread among her merchants and tradesmen, by the universal association of these colonies, at the time of the *stamp-act,* not to import any of her MANUFACTURES. In the year 1718, the Russians and Swedes entered into an agreement, not to suffer Great Britain to export any naval stores from their dominions, but in Russian or Swedish ships, and at their own prices. Great Britain was distressed. *Pitch* and *tar* rose to *three pounds* a barrel. At length she thought of getting these articles from the colonies; and the attempt succeeding, they fell down to fifteen shillings. In the year 1756, Great Britain was threatened with an invasion: An easterly wind blowing for six weeks, she could not MAN her fleet; and the whole nation was thrown into the utmost consternation. The wind changed. The American ships arrived. The fleet sailed in ten or fifteen days. There are some other reflections on this subject worthy of the most deliberate attention of the British parliament; but they are of such a nature that I do not chuse to mention them publicly. I thought I discharged my duty to my country, by taking the liberty, in the year 1765, while the *stamp-act* was in suspence, of writing my sentiments to a man of the greatest influence at home, who afterwards distinguished himself by espousing our cause in the debates concerning the repeal of that act.'

"When we review a performance well written, and founded upon laudable principles, if we do not restrain ourselves to a general approbation, which may be given in few words, the article will unavoidably contain more from the author of it, than from ourselves; this, if any excuse is needful for enabling our Readers, in some measure, to judge for themselves, is pleaded as an apology for our copious extracts from these excellent letters. [lxvii] To conclude; if *reason* is to decide between us and our colonies, in the affairs here controverted, our Author, whose name the advertisements inform us is Dickenson,[2] will not perhaps easily meet with a satisfactory refutation."

LETTERS
FROM
A FARMER.

LETTERS
FROM
A FARMER in *Pennsylvania*,
To the INHABITANTS
OF THE
BRITISH COLONIES.

BOSTON:
PRINTED BY MEIN AND FLEEMING, AND TO
BE SOLD BY JOHN MEIN, AT THE
LONDON BOOK-STORE, NORTH-SIDE
OF KING-STREET.
M DCC LXVIII.

LETTERS
FROM
A FARMER.

LETTER I.

My Dear Countrymen,

I am a farmer, settled after a variety of fortunes, near the banks, of the river *Delaware*, in the province of *Pennsylvania*. I received a liberal education, and have been engaged in the busy scenes of life: But am now convinced, that a man may be as happy without bustle, as with it. My farm is small, my servants are few, and good; I have a little money at interest; I wish for no more: my employment in my own affairs is easy; and with a contented grateful mind, I am compleating the number of days allotted to me by divine goodness.

Being master of my time, I spend a good deal of it in a library, which I think the most valuable part of my small estate; and[6] being acquainted with two or three gentlemen of abilities and learning, who honour me with their friendship, I believe I have acquired a greater share of knowledge in history, and the laws and constitution of my country, than is generally attained by men of my class, many of them not being so fortunate as I have been in the opportunities of getting information.

From infancy I was taught to love humanity and liberty. Inquiry and experience have since confirmed my reverence for the lessons then given me, by convincing me more fully of their truth and excellence. Benevolence towards mankind excites wishes for their welfare, and such wishes endear the means of fulfilling them. Those can be found in liberty alone, and therefore her sacred cause ought to be espoused by every man, on every occasion, to the utmost of his power: as a charitable but poor person does not withhold his *mite*, because he cannot relieve *all* the distresses of the miserable, so let not any honest man suppress his sentiments concerning freedom, however small their influence is likely to be. Perhaps he may "[8]touch some wheel" that will have an effect greater than he expects.

These being my sentiments, I am encouraged to offer to you, my countrymen, my thoughts on some late transactions, that in[7] my opinion are of the utmost importance to you. Conscious of my defects, I have waited some time, in expectation of seeing the subject treated by persons much better qualified for the task; but being therein disappointed, and apprehensive that longer delays will be injurious, I venture at length to request the attention of the public, praying only for one thing,—that is that these lines may be *read* with the same zeal for the happiness of British America, with which they were *wrote*.

With a good deal of surprise I have observed, that little notice has been taken of an act of parliament, as injurious in its principle to the liberties of these colonies, as theSTAMP-ACT was: I mean the act for suspending the legislation of New-York.

The assembly of that government complied with a former act of parliament, requiring certain provisions to be made for the troops in America, in every particular, I think, except the articles of salt, pepper, and vinegar. In my opinion they acted imprudently, considering all circumstances, in not complying so far, as would have given satisfaction, as several colonies did: but my dislike of their conduct in that instance, has not blinded me so much, that I cannot plainly perceive, that they have been punished in a manner pernicious to American freedom, and justly alarming to all the colonies.

[8]

If the BRITISH PARLIAMENT has a legal authority to order, that we shall furnish a single article for the troops here, and to compel obedience to that order; they have the same right to order us to supply those troops with arms, cloaths, and every necessary, and to compel obedience to that order also; in short, to lay *any burdens* they please upon us. What is this but *taxing* us at a *certain sum*, and leaving to us only the *manner* of raising it? How is this mode more tolerable than the STAMP ACT? Would that act have appeared more pleasing to AMERICANS, if being ordered thereby to raise the sum total of the taxes, the mighty privilege had been left to them, of saying how much should be paid for an instrument of writing on paper, and how much for another on parchment?

An act of parliament commanding us to do a certain thing, if it has any validity, is a tax upon us for the expence that accrues in complying with it, and for this reason, I believe, every colony on the continent, that chose to give a mark of their respect forGREAT-BRITAIN, in complying with the act relating to the troops, cautiously avoided the mention of that act, lest their conduct should be attributed to its supposed obligation.

The matter being thus stated, the assembly of *New-York* either had, or had not a right to refuse submission to that act. If they[9] had, and I imagine no AMERICAN will say, they had not, then the parliament had no *right* to compel them to execute it.—If they had not*that right*, they had *no right* to punish them for not executing it; and therefore had *no right* to suspend their legislation, which is a punishment. In fact, if the people of *New-York* cannot be legally taxed but by their own representatives, they cannot be legally deprived of the privileges of making laws, only for insisting on that exclusive privilege of taxation. If they may be legally deprived in such a case of the privilege of making laws, why may they not, with equal reason, be deprived of every other privilege? Or why may not every colony be treated in the same manner, when any of them shall dare to deny their assent to any impositions that shall be directed? Or what signifies the repeal of the STAMP-ACT, if these colonies are to lose their *other* privileges, by not tamely surrendering that of *taxation*?

There is one consideration arising from this suspicion, which is not generally attended to, but shews its importance very clearly. It was not *necessary* that this suspension should be caused by an act of parliament. The crown might have restrained the governor of *New-York*, even from calling the assembly together, by its prerogative in the royal governments. This step, I suppose, would have[10] been taken, if the conduct of the assembly of *New-York*, had been regarded as an act of disobedience *to the crown alone*: but it is regarded as an act of "disobedience to the authority of the BRITISH LEGISLATURE." This gives the suspension a consequence vastly more affecting. It is a parliamentary assertion of the *supreme authority* of the *British legislature* over these colonies in *the part of taxation*; and is intended to COMPEL *New-York* unto a submission to that authority. It seems therefore to me as much a violation of the liberty of the people of that province, and consequently of all these colonies, as if the parliament had sent a number of regiments to be quartered upon them till they should comply. For it is evident, that the suspension is meant as a compulsion; and the *method* of compelling is totally indifferent. It is indeed probable, that the sight of red coats, and the beating of drums would have been most alarming, because people are generally more influenced by their eyes and ears than by their reason: But whoever seriously considers the matter, must perceive, that a dreadful stroke is aimed at the liberty of these colonies: For the cause of *one* is the cause of *all*. If the parliament may lawfully deprive *New-York* of any of its rights, it may deprive any, or all the other colonies of their rights; and nothing can possibly so much encourage such attempts, as a mutual inattention to the interest[11] of each other. *To divide, and thus to destroy,* is the first political maxim in attacking those who are powerful by their union. He certainly is not a wise man, who folds his arms and reposeth himself at home, seeing with unconcern the flames that have invaded his neighbour's house, without any endeavours to extinguish them. When Mr. *Hampden's*ship-money cause, for three shillings and four-pence, was tried, all the people of*England*, with anxious expectation, interested themselves in the important decision; and when the slightest point touching the freedom of a single colony is agitated, I earnestly wish, that all the rest may with equal ardour support their sister. Very much may be said on this subject, but I hope, more at present is unnecessary.

With concern I have observed that two assemblies of this province have sat and adjourned, without taking any notice of this act. It may perhaps be asked, what would have been proper for them to do? I am by no means fond of inflammatory measures. I detest them.——I should be sorry that any thing should be done which might justly displease our sovereign or our mother-country. But a firm, modest exertion of a free spirit, should never be wanting on public occasions. It appears to me, that it would have been sufficient for the assembly, to have ordered our agents to represent to the King's ministers, their sense of the suspending act, and[12] to pray for its repeal. Thus we should have borne our testimony against it; and might therefore reasonably expect that on a like occasion, we might receive the same assistance from the other colonies.

"*Concordia res parvæ crescunt.*"
Small things grow great by concord.——

A FARMER.

[13]
LETTER II.

Beloved Countrymen,

There is another late act of parliament, which seems to me to be as destructive to the liberty of these colonies, as that inserted in my last letter; that is, the act for granting the duties on paper, glass, &c. It appears to me to be unconstitutional.

The parliament unquestionably possesses a legal authority to *regulate* the trade of*Great-Britain*, and all its colonies. Such an authority is essential to the relation between a mother country and its colonies; and necessary for the common good of all. He, who considers these provinces as states distinct from the *British Empire*, has very slender notions of *justice* or of *their interests*. We are but parts of *a whole*; and therefore there must exist a power somewhere, to preside, and preserve the connection in due order. This power is lodged in the parliament; and we are as much dependant on *Great-Britain*, as a perfectly free people can be on another.

I have looked over every *statute* relating to these colonies, from their first settlement[14]to this time; and I find every one of them founded on this principle, till the STAMP-ACTadministration[2]. *All before* are calculated to preserve or promote a mutually beneficial intercourse between the several constituent parts of the empire;[15] and though many of them imposed duties on trade, yet those duties were always imposed *with design* to restrain the commerce of one part, that was injurious to another, and thus to promote the general welfare. The raising a revenue thereby was[16] never intended. Thus, the king by his judges in his courts of justice, imposes fines, which all together amount to a considerable sum, and contribute to the support of government: but this is merely a consequence arising from restrictions, which only meant to[17] keep peace, and prevent confusion; and surely a man would argue very loosely, who should conclude from hence, that the King has a right to levy money in general upon his subjects; Never did the *British parliament*, till the period abovementioned, think of imposing duties in America FOR THE PURPOSE OF RAISING A REVENUE. Mr. *Greenville's* sagacity first introduced this language, in the preamble to the 4th of Geo. III. Ch. 15, which has these words—"And whereas it is just and necessary that a REVENUE BE RAISED IN YOUR MAJESTY'S SAID DOMINIONS IN AMERICA, *for defraying the expences of defending, protecting and securing the same*: We your Majesty's most dutiful and loyal subjects,THE COMMONS OF GREAT BRITAIN, in parliament assembled,[18] being desirous to make some provision in the present session of parliament, towards raising the said revenue in America, have resolved to give and grant unto your Majesty the several rates and duties herein after mentioned," &c.

A few months after came the *Stamp-act*, which reciting this, proceeds in the same strange mode of expression, thus—"And whereas it is just and necessary, that provision be made FOR RAISING A FURTHER REVENUE WITHIN YOUR MAJESTY'S DOMINIONS IN AMERICA, towards defraying the said expences, we your Majesty's most dutiful and loyal subjects, the COMMONS OF GREAT-BRITAIN, &c. GIVE and GRANT," &c. as before.

The last act, granting duties upon paper, &c. carefully pursues these modern precedents. The preamble is, "Whereas it is expedient that a revenue should be raised in your Majesty's dominions in America, for making a more certain and adequate provision for the defraying the charge of the administration of justice, and the support of civil government in such provinces, where it shall be found necessary; and towards the further defraying the expences of defending, protecting and securing the said dominions, we your Majesty's most dutiful and loyal subjects, the COMMONS OF GREAT-BRITAIN, &c. give and grant," &c. as before.

Here we may observe an authority *expressly* claimed to impose duties on these colonies;[19] not for the regulation of trade; not for the preservation or promotion of a mutually beneficial intercourse between the several constituent parts of the empire, heretofore the *sole objects* of parliamentary institutions; *but for the single purpose of levying money upon us.*

This I call an[10] innovation; and a most dangerous innovation. It may perhaps be objected, that *Great-Britain* has a right to lay what duties she pleases upon her[11]exports, and it makes no difference to us, whether they are paid here or there.

To this I answer. These colonies require many things for their use, which the laws of*Great-Britain* prohibit them from getting any where but from her. Such are paper and glass.

[20]

That we may be legally bound to pay any *general* duties on these commodities, relative to the regulation of trade, is granted; but we being *obliged by her laws* to take them from Great Britain, any *special* duties imposed on their exportation *to us only, with intention to raise a revenue from us only*, are as much *taxes* upon us, as those imposed by the *Stamp-act*.

What is the difference in *substance* and *right*, whether the same sum is raised upon us by the rates mentioned in the Stamp-act, on the *use* of the paper, or by these duties, on the *importation* of it. It is nothing but the edition of a former book, with a new title page.

Suppose the duties were made payable in *Great-Britain*?

It signifies nothing to us, whether they are to be paid here or there. Had the *Stamp-act*directed, that all the paper should be landed in *Florida*, and the duties paid there, before it was brought to the *British Colonies*, would the act have raised less money upon us, or have been less destructive of our rights? By no means: For as we were under a necessity of using the paper, we should have been under the necessity of paying the duties. Thus, in the present case, a like *necessity* will subject us, if this act continues in force, to the payment of the duties now imposed.

[21]

Why was the *Stamp-act* then so pernicious to freedom? It did not enact, that every man in the colonies *should* buy a certain quantity of paper—No: It only directed, that no instrument of writing should be valid in law, if not made on stamp paper, &c.

The makers of that act knew full well, that the confusions that would arise upon the disuse of writings would COMPEL the colonies to use the stamp paper, and therefore to pay the taxes imposed. For this reason the *Stamp-act* was said to be a law THAT WOULD EXECUTE ITSELF. For the very same reason, the last act of parliament, if it is granted to have any force here, will execute itself, and will be attended with the very same consequences to *American Liberty*.

Some persons perhaps may say, that this act lays us under no necessity to pay the duties imposed, because we may ourselves manufacture the articles on which they are laid: whereas by the Stamp-act no instrument of writing could be good, unless made on British paper, and that too stampt.

Such an objection amounts to no more than this, that the injury resulting to these colonies, from the total disuse of British paper and glass, will not be *so afflicting* as that which would have resulted from the total disuse of writing among them; for by that means even the stamp-act might have been eluded. Why then was it universally detested[22]by them as slavery itself? Because it presented to these devoted provinces nothing but a choice of calamities, imbittered by indignities, each of which it was unworthy of freemen to bear. But is no injury a violation of right but the *greatest* injury? If the eluding the payment of the duties imposed by the stamp-act, would have subjected us to a more dreadful inconvenience, than the eluding the payment of those imposed by the late act; does it therefore follow, that the last is no violation of our rights, though it is calculated for the same purpose that the other was, that is, *to raise money upon us*,WITHOUT OUR CONSENT?

This would be making *right* to consist, not in an exemption from *injury*, but from a certain *degree of injury*.

But the objectors may further say, that we shall sustain no injury at all by the disuse of British paper and glass. We might not, if we could make as much as we want. But can any man, acquainted with America, believe this possible? I am told there are but two or three *glass-houses* on this continent, and but very few *paper-mills*; and suppose more should be erected, a long course of years must elapse, before they can be brought to perfection. This continent is a country of planters, farmers, and fishermen; not of manufacturers. The difficulty of establishing particular manufactures in such a country, is almost insuperable,[23] for one manufacture is connected with others in such a manner, that it may be said to be impossible to establish one or two, without establishing several others. The experience of many nations may convince us of this truth.

Inexpressible therefore must be our distresses in evading the late acts, by the disuse of British paper and glass. Nor will this be the extent of our misfortunes, if we admit the legality of that act.

Great-Britain has prohibited the manufacturing iron and steel in these colonies, without any objection being made to her right of doing it. The like right she must have to prohibit any other manufacture among us. Thus she is possessed of an undisputed*precedent* on that point. This authority, she will say, is founded on the *original intention*of settling these colonies; that is, that she should manufacture for them, and that they should supply her with materials. The *equity* of this policy, she will also say, has been universally acknowledged by the colonies, who never have made the least objection to statutes for that purpose; and will further appear by the *mutual benefits* flowing from this usage, ever since the settlement of these colonies.

Our great advocate, Mr. PITT, in his speeches on the debate concerning the repeal of the *Stamp-act*, acknowledged, that Great-Britain could restrain our manufactures. His[24]words are these—"This kingdom, as the supreme governing and legislative power, has*always* bound the colonies by her regulations and *restrictions* in trade, in navigation, in*manufactures*——in every thing, *except that of taking their money out of their pockets*,WITHOUT THEIR CONSENT." Again he says, "We may bind their trade, CONFINE THEIR MANUFACTURES, and exercise every power whatever, except that of taking money out of their pockets, WITHOUT THEIR CONSENT."

Here then, let my countrymen, ROUSE yourselves, and behold the ruin hanging over their heads. If they ONCE admit, that Great-Britain may lay duties upon her exportations to us, *for the purpose of levying money on us only*, she then will have nothing to do, but to lay those duties on the articles which she prohibits us to manufacture—and the tragedy of American liberty is finished. We have been prohibited from procuring manufactures, in all cases, any where but from Great-Britain, (excepting linens, which we are permitted to import directly from Ireland). We have been prohibited, in some cases, from manufacturing for ourselves; We are therefore exactly in the situation of a city besieged, which is surrounded by the works of the besiegers in every part *but one*. If *that* is closed up, no step can be taken, *but to surrender at discretion*. If Great-Britain can order us to come to her for necessaries we[25] want, and can order us to pay what taxes she pleases before we take them away, or when we have them here, we are as abject slaves, as France and Poland can shew in wooden shoes, and with uncombed hair.[12]

Perhaps the nature of the necessities of the dependant states, caused by the policy of a governing one, for her own benefit, may be elucidated by a fact mentioned in history. When the Carthaginians were possessed of the island of Sardinia, they made a decree, that the Sardinians should not get corn, any other way than from the Carthaginians. Then, by imposing any duties they would, they drained from the miserable Sardinians any sums they pleased; and whenever that oppressed people made the least movement to assert their liberty, their tyrants starved them to death or submission. This may be called the most perfect kind of political necessity.

From what has been said, I think this uncontrovertible conclusion may be deduced, that when a ruling state obliges a dependant state to take certain commodities from her alone, it is implied in the nature of that obligation; and is essentially requisite to give it the least degree of justice; and is inseparably[26] united with it, in order to preserve any share of freedom to the dependant state; that those commodities should never be loaded with duties for the sole purpose of levying money on the dependant state.

The place of paying the duties imposed by the late act, appears to me therefore to be totally immaterial. The single question is, whether the parliament can legally impose duties to be paid *by the people of these colonies only* FOR THE SOLE PURPOSE OF RAISING A REVENUE, *on commodities which she obliges us to take from her alone*; or, in other words, whether the parliament can legally take money out of our pockets, without our consent. If they can, our boasted liberty is but

Vox et præterea nihil.
A sound, and nothing else.

A FARMER.

[27]

LETTER III.

Beloved Countrymen,

I rejoice to find, that my two former letters to you, have been generally received with so much favour by such of you whose sentiments I have had an opportunity of knowing. Could you look into my heart, you would instantly perceive an ardent affection for your persons, a zealous attachment to your interests, a lively resentment of every insult and injury offered to your honour or happiness, and an inflexible resolution to assert your rights, to the utmost of my weak power, to be the only motives that have engaged me to address you.

I am no further concerned in any thing affecting America, than any one of you, and when liberty leaves it I can quit it much more conveniently than most of you: but while divine providence, that gave me existence in a land of freedom, permits my head to think, my lips to speak, and my hand to move, I shall so highly and gratefully value the blessing received, as to take care that my silence and inactivity shall not give my implied assent to any act degrading my brethren and myself from the birthright[28]wherewith heaven itself "*hath made us free.*[1]"

Sorry I am to learn, that there are some few persons, shake their heads with solemn motion, and pretend to wonder what can be the meaning of these letters. "Great-Britain, they say, is too powerful to contend with; she is determined to oppress us; it is in vain to speak of right on one side, when there is power on the other; when we are strong enough to resist, we shall attempt it; but now we are not strong enough, and therefore we had better be quiet; it signifies nothing to convince us that our rights are invaded, when we cannot defend them, and if we should get into riots and tumults about the late act, it will only draw down heavier displeasure upon us."

What can such men design? What do their grave observations amount to, but this— "that these colonies, totally regardless of their liberties, should commit them, with humble resignation, to *chance, time,* and the tender mercies of *ministers.*"

Are these men ignorant, that usurpations, which might have been successfully opposed at first, acquire strength by continuance, and thus become irresistible? Do they condemn the conduct of these colonies, concerning the *Stamp-act*? Or have they forgot its successful issue? Ought the colonies at that[29] time, instead of acting as they did, to have trusted for relief, to the fortuitous events of futurity? If it is needless "to speak of rights"

23

now, it was as needless then. If the behaviour of the colonies was prudent and glorious then, and successful too; it will be equally prudent and glorious to act in the same manner now, if our rights are equally invaded, and may be as successful. Therefore it becomes necessary to enquire, whether "our rights *are* invaded." To talk of "defending" them, as if they could be no otherwise "defended" than by arms, is as much out of the way, as if a man having a choice of several roads to reach his journey's end, should prefer the worst, for no other reason, than because it is the worst.

As to "riots and tumults," the gentlemen who are so apprehensive of them, are much mistaken, if they think, that grievances cannot be redressed without such assistance.

I will now tell the gentlemen, what is "the meaning of these letters." The meaning of them is, to convince the people of these colonies, that they are at this moment exposed to the most imminent dangers; and to persuade them immediately, vigorously, and unanimously, to exert themselves, in the most firm, but most peaceable manner for obtaining relief.

The cause of liberty is a cause of too much dignity, to be sullied by turbulence[30] and tumult. It ought to be maintained in a manner suitable to her nature. Those who engage in it, should breathe a sedate, yet fervent spirit, animating them to actions of prudence, justice, modesty, bravery, humanity, and magnanimity.

To such a wonderful degree were the antient *Spartans*, as brave and as free a people as ever existed, inspired by this happy temperature of soul, that rejecting even in their battles the use of trumpets, and other instruments for exciting heat and rage, they marched up to scenes of havock and horror, with the sound of flutes, to the tunes of which their steps kept pace—"exhibiting, as *Plutarch* says, at once a terrible and delightful sight, and proceeding with a deliberate valour, full of hope and good assurance, as if some divinity had insensibly assisted them."

I hope, my dear countrymen, that you will in every colony be upon your guard against those who may at any time endeavour to stir you up, under pretences of patriotism, to any measures disrespectful to our sovereign and our mother country. Hot, rash, disorderly proceedings, injure the reputation of a people as to wisdom, valour and virtue, without procuring them the least benefit. I pray God, that he may be pleased to inspire you and your posterity to the latest ages with that spirit, of which I have an idea, but find a difficulty to express: to express in[31] the best manner I can, I mean a spirit that shall so guide you, that it will be impossible to determine, whether an *American*'s character is most distinguishable for his loyalty to his sovereign, his duty to his mother country, his love of freedom, or his affection for his native soil.

Every government, at some time or other, falls into wrong measures; these may proceed from mistake or passion.——But every such measure does not dissolve the obligation between the governors and the governed; the mistake may be corrected; the passion may pass over.

It is the duty of the governed, to endeavour to rectify the mistake, and appease the passion. They have not at first any other right, than to represent their grievances, and to pray for redress, unless an emergency is so pressing, as not to allow time for receiving an answer to their applications which rarely happens. If their applications are disregarded, then that kind of opposition becomes justifiable, which can be made without breaking the laws, or disturbing the public peace. This consists in the prevention of the oppressors reaping advantage from their oppressions, and not in their punishment. For experience may teach them what reason did not; and harsh methods, cannot be proper, till milder ones have failed.

If at length it becomes undoubted, that an inveterate resolution is formed to annihilate[32]the liberties of the governed, the English history affords frequent examples of resistance by force. What particular circumstances will in any future case justify such resistance, can never be ascertained till they happen. Perhaps it may be allowable to say, generally, that it never can be justifiable, until the people are FULLY CONVINCED, that any further submission will be destructive to their happiness.

When the appeal is made to the sword, highly probable it is, that the punishment will exceed the offence; and the calamities attending on war out weigh those preceding it. These considerations of justice and prudence, will always have great influence with good and wise men.

To these reflections on this subject, it remains to be added, and ought for ever to be remembered; that resistance in the case of colonies against their mother country, is extremely different from the resistance of a people against their prince. A nation may change their King or race of Kings, and retain their antient form of government, be gainers by changing. Thus Great-Britain, under the illustrious house of Brunswick, a house that seems to flourish for the happiness of mankind, has found a felicity, unknown in the reigns of the Stuarts. But if once we are separated from our mother country, what new form of government shall we accept, or when shall we find another Britain to supply[33] our loss? Torn from the body to which we are united by religion, liberty, laws, affections, relations, language, and commerce, we must bleed at every vein.

In truth, the prosperity of these provinces is founded in their dependance on Great-Britain; and when she returns to "her old good humour, and old good nature," as Lord Clerendon expresses it, I hope they will always esteem it their duty and interest, as it most certainly will be, to promote her welfare by all the means in their power.

We cannot act with too much caution in our disputes. Anger produces anger; and differences that might be accommodated by kind and respectful behaviour, may by imprudence be changed to an incurable rage.

In quarrels between countries, as well as in those between individuals, when they have risen to a certain heighth, the first cause of dissention is no longer remembred, the minds of the parties being wholly engaged in recollecting and resenting the mutual expressions of their dislike. When feuds have reached that fatal point, all considerations of reason and equity vanish; and a blind fury governs, or rather confounds all things. A people no longer regards their interest, but the gratification of their wrath. The sway of the Cleon's,[14] and Clodius's, the designing[34] and detestable flatters of the prevailing passion, becomes confirmed.

Wise and good men in vain oppose the storm, and may think themselves fortunate, if, endeavouring to preserve their ungrateful fellow citizens, they do not ruin themselves. Their prudence will be called baseness; their moderation, guilt; and if their virtue does not lead them to destruction, as that of many other great and excellent persons has done, they may survive, to receive from their expiring country, the mournful glory of her acknowledgment, that their councils, if regarded, would have saved her.

The constitutional modes of obtaining relief, are those which I would wish to see pursued on the present occasion, that is, by petitioning of our assemblies, or, where they are not permitted to meet, of the people to the powers that can afford us relief.

We have an excellent prince, in whose good dispositions towards us we may confide. We have a generous, sensible, and humane nation, to whom we may apply. They may be deceived: they may, by artful men, be provoked to anger against us; but I cannot yet believe they will be cruel or unjust; or that their anger will be implacable. Let us behave like dutiful children, who have received unmerited blows from a beloved parent. Let us complain to our parents; but let our complaints speak at the same[35] time, the language of affliction and veneration.

If, however, it shall happen by an unfortunate course of affairs, that our applications to his Majesty and the parliament for the redress, prove ineffectual, let us then take another step, by withholding from Great-Britain, all the advantages she has been used to receive from us. Then let us try, if our ingenuity, industry, and frugality, will not give weight to our remonstrances. Let us all be united with one spirit in one cause. Let us invent; let us work; let us save; let us at the same time, keep up our claims, and unceasingly repeat our complaints; but above all, let us implore the protection of that infinite good and gracious Being, "by whom kings reign and princes decree justice."

"*Nil desperandum.*"

Nothing is to be despaired of.

A FARMER.

[36]

[37]

LETTER IV.

Beloved Countrymen,

An objection, I hear, has been made against what I offer in my second letter, which I would willingly clear up before I proceed. "There is," say these objectors "a material difference between the Stamp-act and the late act for laying a duty on paper, &c. that justifies the conduct of those who opposed the former, and yet are willing to submit to the latter. The duties imposed by the Stamp-act, were internal taxes, but the present are external, which therefore the parliament may have a right to impose."——To this I answer, with a total denial of the power of parliament to lay upon these colonies any tax whatever.

This point being so important to this and to all succeeding generations, I wish to be clearly understood.

To the word "Tax," I annex that meaning which the constitution and history of England require to be annexed to it; that it is, an imposition on the subject for the sole purpose of levying money.

In the early ages of our monarchy, the services rendered to the crown, for the[38] general good, were personal;[15] but in progress of time, such institutions being found inconvenient, certain gifts and grants of their own property were made by the people, under the several names of aids, tallages, talks, taxes, subsidies, &c. These were made as may be collected even from the names for public service, "upon need and necessity,"[16] all these sums were levied upon the people by virtue of their voluntary gift.[17] The design of them was to support[39] the national honour and interest. Some of those grants comprehended duties arising from trade, being imports on merchandizes. These Chief Justice Coke classes "under subsides"[18] and "parliamentary aids." They are also called "customs." But whatever the name was, they were always considered as gifts of the people to the crown, to be employed for public uses.

Commerce was at a low ebb, and most surprising instances may be produced, how little it was attended to, for a succession of ages. The terms that have been mentioned, and among the rest that of "tax," had[40] obtained a national, parliamentary meaning, drawn from the principles of the constitution, long before any Englishmen thought of regulations of trade "by imposing duties."

Whenever we speak of taxes among Englishmen, let us therefore speak of them with reference to the intentions with which, and the principles on which they have been established. This will give certainty to our expression, and safety to our conduct: but if when we have in view the liberty of these colonies, and the influence of "taxes" laid without our consent, we proceed in any other course, we pursue a Juno[19] indeed, but shall only catch a cloud.

In the national parliamentary sense insisted on, the word "tax"[20] was certainly understood by the congress at New-York, whose resolves may be said to form the American "bill of rights." I am satisfied that the congress was of opinion, that no impositions could be legally laid on the people of these colonies for the purpose of levying money, but by themselves or their representatives.

The third, fourth, fifth, and sixth resolves are thus expressed.

[41]

III. "That it is inseparably essential to the freedom of a people and the undoubted right of Englishmen, that no tax be imposed on them, but with their own consent, given personally or by their representatives."

IV. "That the people of the colonies are not, and from their local circumstances cannot be represented in the House of Commons, in Great-Britain."

V. "That the only representatives of the people of the colonies, are the persons chosen therein by themselves; and that no taxes ever have been, or can be constitutionally imposed on them, but by their respective legislatures."

VI. "That all supplies to the crown being free gifts of the people, it is unreasonable and inconsistent with the principles and spirit of the British constitution, for the people of Great-Britain to grant to his Majesty the property of the colonies."

Here is no distinction made, between internal and external taxes. It is evident from the short reasoning thrown into these resolves that every imposition "to grant to his Majesty the property of the colonies," was thought a "tax;" and that every such imposition if laid any other way "but with their consent, given personally, or by their representatives;" was not only "unreasonable, and inconsistent with the principles and spirit of the British constitution,"[42] but destructive "to the freedom of a people."

This language is clear and important. A "tax" means an imposition to raise money. Such persons therefore as speak of internal and external "taxes," I pray may pardon me, if I object to that expression as applied to the privileges and interests of these colonies. There may be external and internal impositions, founded on different principles, and having different tendencies; every "tax" being an imposition, tho' every imposition is not a "tax." But all "taxes" are founded on the same principle, and have the same tendency.

"External impositions for the regulation of our trade, do not grant to his Majesty the property of the colonies." They only prevent the colonies acquiring property in things not necessary, and in a manner judged to be injurious to the welfare of the whole empire. But the last statute respecting us, "grants to his Majesty the property of these colonies," by laying duties on manufactures of Great-Britain, which they must take, and which he settled them, in order that they should take.

What[21] "tax" can be more "internal" than this? Here is money drawn without[43] their consent from a society, who have constantly enjoyed a constitutional mode of raising all money among themselves. The payment of this tax they have no possible method of avoiding, as they cannot do without the commodities on which it is laid, and[44] they cannot manufacture these commodities themselves; besides, if this unhappy country should be so lucky as to elude this act, by getting parchment enough to use in the place of paper, or reviving the antient method of writing on wax and bark, and by inventing something to serve instead of glass, her ingenuity would stand her in little stead; for then the parliament would have nothing to do, but to prohibit manufactures, or to lay a tax on hats and woollen cloths, which they have already prohibited the colonies from supplying each other with; or on instruments and tools of steel and iron, which they have prohibited the provincials[45] from manufacturing at all[22] And then what little gold and silver they have, must be torn from their hands, or they will not be able in a short time, to get an ax[23] for cutting their firewood, nor a plough for raising their food.—In what respect therefore, I beg leave to ask, is the late act preferable to the Stamp-act, or more consistent with the liberties of the colonies? "I regard them both with equal apprehension, and think they ought to be in the same manner opposed."

"*Habemus quidem senatus consultum—tanquam gladium in vagina repositum*" We have a statute like a sword in the scabbard.

A FARMER.

[46]

[47]

LETTER V.

Beloved Countrymen,

Perhaps the objection to the late act, imposing duties upon paper, &c. might have been safely rested on the arguments drawn from the universal conduct of parliaments and ministers, from the first existence of these colonies, to the administration of Mr. Grenville.

What but the indisputable, the acknowledged exclusive right of the colonies to tax themselves, could be the reason, that in this long period of more than one hundred and fifty years, no statute was ever passed for the sole purpose of raising a revenue on the colonies? And how clear, how cogent must that reason be, to which every parliament and every minister, for so long a time submitted, without a single attempt to innovate?

England in part of that course of years, and Great Britain, in other parts, was engaged in fierce and expensive wars; troubled with some tumultuous and bold parliaments; governed by many daring and wicked ministers; yet none of them ever ventured to touch the PALLADIUM OF AMERICAN LIBERTY. Ambition, avarice, faction, tyranny, all revered it. Whenever it was necessary[48] to raise money on the colonies, the requisitions of the crown were made, and dutifully complied with. The parliament from time to time regulated their trade, and that of the rest of the empire, to preserve their dependencies, and the connection of the whole in good order.

The people of Great-Britain in support of their privileges, boast much of their antiquity. Yet it may well be questioned, if there is a single privilege of a British subject, supported by longer, more solemn, or more uninterrupted testimony, than the exclusive right of taxation in these colonies. The people of Great-Britain consider that kingdom as the sovereign of these colonies, and would now annex to that sovereignty a prerogative never heard of before. How would they bear this, was the case their own? What would they think of a new prerogative claimed by the crown? We may guess what their conduct would be from the transports of passion into which they fell about the late embargo, laid to remove the most emergent necessities of state, admitting of no delay; and for which there were numerous precedents. Let our liberties be treated with the same tenderness, and it is all we desire.

Explicit as the conduct of parliaments, for so many ages, is, to prove that no money can be levied on these colonies, by parliament for the purpose of raising a revenue; yet it is not the only evidence in our favour.

[49]

Every one of the most material arguments against the legality of the Stamp-act operates with equal force against the act now objected to; but as they are well known, it seems unnecessary to repeat them here.

This general one only shall be considered at present. That tho' these colonies are dependant on Great-Britain; and tho' she has a legal power to make laws for preserving that dependance; yet it is not necessary for this purpose, nor essential to the relation between a mother-country and her colonies, as was eagerly contended by the advocates for the Stamp-act, that she should raise money upon them without their consent.

Colonies were formerly planted by warlike nations, to keep their enemies in awe; to relieve their country overburthened with inhabitants; or to discharge a number of discontented and troublesome citizens. But in more modern ages, the spirit of violence being in some measure, if the expression may be allowed, sheathed in commerce, colonies have been settled by the nations of Europe for the purposes of trade. These purposes were to be attained by the colonies raising for their mother country those things which she did not produce herself; and by supplying themselves from her with things they wanted. These were the national objects in the commencement of our colonies, and have been uniformly so in their promotion.

[50]

To answer these grand purposes, perfect liberty was known to be necessary; all history proving, that trade and freedom are nearly related to each other. By a due regard to this wise and just plan, the infant colonies exposed in the unknown climates, and unexplored wildernesses of this new world, lived, grew, and flourished.

The parent country with undeviating prudence and virtue, attentive to the first principles of colonization, drew to herself the benefits she might reasonably expect, and preserved to her children the blessings, on which those benefits were founded. She made laws obliging her colonies to carry to her all those products which she wanted for her own use; and all those raw materials which she chose herself to work up. Besides this restriction, she forbade them to procure manufactures from any other part of the globe; or even the products of European countries, which alone could rival her, without being first brought to her. In short, by a variety of laws, she regulated their trade in such a manner, as she thought most conducive to their mutual advantage, and her own welfare. A power was reserved to the crown of repealing any laws that should be enacted. The executive authority of government was all lodged in the crown and its representatives; and an appeal was secured to the crown from all judgments in the administration of justice.

[51]

For all these powers established by the mother country over the colonies; for all these immense emoluments derived by her from them; for all their difficulties and distresses in fixing themselves, what was the recompense made them? A communication of her rights in general, and particularly of that great one, the foundation of all the rest—that their property, acquired with so much pain and hazard, should not be disposed of by[24]any one but themselves—or to use the beautiful and emphatic language of the sacred scriptures, "that they should sit every man under his vine, and under his fig tree, and none should make them afraid."[25]

Can any man of candour and knowledge deny, that these institutions, form an affinity between Great-Britain and her colonies, that sufficiently secures their dependance upon her? or that for her to levy taxes upon them, is to reverse the nature of things? or that she can pursue such a measure, without reducing them to a state of vassalage?

If any person cannot conceive the supremacy of Great Britain to exist, without the power of laying taxes to levy money upon us, the history of the colonies and of Great-Britain since their settlement will prove the contrary. He will there find the amazing[52]advantages arising to her from them—The constant exercise of her supremacy—and their filial submission to it, without a single rebellion, or even the thought of one, from the first emigration to this moment—and all these things have happened, without an instance of Great-Britain laying taxes to levy money upon them.

How many British authors[26] have remonstrated[53] that the present wealth, power and glory of their country are founded on these colonies? As constantly as streams tend to the ocean, have they been pouring the fruits of all their labours into their mother's lap. Good Heaven! And shall a total oblivion of[54] former tendernesses and blessings be spread over the minds of a wise people, by the sordid acts of intriguing men, who covering their selfish projects under pretences of public good, first enrage their countrymen into a frenzy of passion, and then advance their[55] own influence and interest, by gratifying that passion, which they themselves have barely excited?

Hitherto Great-Britain has been contented with her prosperity. Moderation has been the rule of her conduct. But now a generous and humane people that so often has[56]protected the liberty of strangers, is inflamed into an attempt to tear a privilege from her own children, which, if executed, must in their opinion, sink them into slaves: And for what? For a pernicious power, not necessary to her, as her own experience may[57]convince her; but horribly dreadful and detestable to them.

It seems extremely probable, that when cool, dispassionate posterity shall consider the affectionate intercourse, the reciprocal benefits, and the unsuspecting confidence,[58]that have subsisted between these colonies and their parent country, for such a length of time, they will execrate with the bitterest curses the infamous memory of those men, whose pestilential ambition, unnecessarily, wantonly, first opened the sources of civil discord, between them; first turned their love into jealousy; and first taught these provinces, filled with grief and anxiety, to enquire,

"*Mens ubi materna est?*"
Where is maternal affection.

A FARMER.

[59]

LETTER VI.

Beloved Countrymen,

It may perhaps be objected against the arguments that have been offered to the public concerning the legal power of the parliament, that it has always exercised the power of imposing duties for the purposes of raising a revenue on the productions of these colonies carried to Great-Britain, which may be called a tax on them. To this I answer; that is no more a violation of the rights of the colonies, than their being ordered to carry certain of their productions to Great-Britain, which is no violation at all; it being implied in the relation between them, that the colonies should not carry such commodities to other nations, as should enable them to interfere with the mother country. The duties imposed on these commodities when brought to her, are only a consequence of her paternal right; and if the point is thoroughly examined, will be found to be laid on the people of the mother country, and not at all dangerous to the liberties of the colonies. Whatever these duties are, they must proportionably raise the price of the goods, and consequently the duties must be paid by the consumers. In this light they were[60] considered by the parliament in the 25 Char. II. Chap.

29

7, sec. 2, which says, that the productions of the plantations were carried from one to another free from all customs "while the subjects of this your kingdom of England have paid great customs and impositions for what of them have been spent here, &c." Such duties therefore can never be injurious to the liberties of the colonies.

Besides, if Great-Britain exports these commodities again, the duties will injure her own trade, so that she cannot hurt us without plainly and immediately hurting herself; and this is our check against her acting arbitrarily in this respect.

It[27] may, perhaps, be further objected, "that it being granted that statutes made[61] for regulating trade are binding upon us, it will be difficult for any persons but the makers of the laws to determine, which of them are made for the regulating of trade, and which for raising a revenue; and that from hence may arise confusion."

To this I answer, that the objection is of no force in the present case, or such as resemble it, because the act now in question is formed expressly for the sole purpose of raising a revenue.

However, supposing the design of the parliament had not been expressed, the objection seems to me of no weight, with regard to the influence, which those who may make[62] it, might expect it ought to have on the conduct of the colonies.

It is true, that impositions for raising a revenue, may be hereafter called regulations of trade, but names will not change the nature of things. Indeed we ought firmly to believe, what is an undoubted truth, confirmed by the unhappy experience of many states heretofore free, that unless the most watchful attention be exerted, a new servitude may be slipped upon us under the sanction of usual and respectable terms.

Thus the Cæsars ruined Roman liberty, under the titles of tribunical and dictatorial authorities,——old and venerable dignities, known in the most flourishing times of freedom. In imitation of the same policy, James II. when he meant to establish popery, talked of liberty of conscience, the most sacred of all liberties; and had thereby almost deceived the dissenters into destruction.

All artful rulers, who strive to extend their own power beyond its just limits, endeavour to give to their attempts, as much semblance of legality as possible. Those who succeed them may venture to go a little farther; for each new encroachment will be strengthened by a former,[28]"That which is now supported by examples, growing old, will become an example itself," and thus support fresh usurpations.
[63]
A free people, therefore, can never be too quick in observing, nor too firm in opposing the beginnings of alterations, either in form or reality, respecting institutions formed for their security. The first leads to the last; on the other hand nothing is more certain, than that forms of liberty may be retained, when the substance is gone. In government as well as in religion, "the letter killeth, but the spirit giveth life."[29]

I will beg leave to enforce this remark by a few instances. The crown, by the constitution, has the prerogative of creating peers; the existence of that order in due number and dignity, is essential to the constitution; and if the crown did not exercise that prerogative, the peerage must have long since decreased so much, as to have lost its proper influence. Suppose a prince for some unjust purposes, should from time to time advance many needy profligate wretches, to that rank, that all the independance of the house of Lords should be destroyed, there would then be a manifest violation of the constitution, under the appearance of using legal prerogative.

The house of Commons claim the privilege of forming all money-bills, and will not suffer either of the other branches of the legislature to add to or alter them; contending that their power, simply extends to an[64] acceptance or rejection of them. This privilege appears to be just; but under pretence of this just privilege, the house of Commons has claimed a licence of tacking to money bills, clauses relating to many things of a totally different kind, and have thus forced them, in a manner, on the crown and lords. This seems to be an abuse of that privilege, and it may be vastly more abused. Suppose a future house; influenced by some displaced discontented demagogues, in a time of danger, should tack to a money bill something so injurious to the king and peers, that they would not assent to it and yet the

Commons should obstinately insist on it; the whole kingdom would be exposed to ruin, *under the appearance of maintaining a valuable privilege.*

In these cases it might be difficult for a while to determine, whether the King intended to exercise his prerogative in a constitutional manner or not; or whether the Commons insisted on the demand factitiously, or for the public good: But surely the conduct of the crown, or of the house, would in time sufficiently explain itself.

Ought not the people therefore to watch to observe facts? to search into causes? to investigate designs? and have they not a right of judging from the evidence before them, on no slighter points than their liberty and happiness? It would be less than trifling, wherever a British government is established, to make use of any other arguments[65] to prove such a right. It is sufficient to remind the reader of the day on which King William landed at Torbay.[30]

I will now apply what has been said to the present question. The nature of any impositions laid by parliament on the colonies, must determine the design in laying them. It may not be easy in every instance to discover that design. Whenever it is doubtful, I think submission cannot be dangerous; nay, it must be right: for, in my opinion, there is no privilege the colonies claim, which they ought, in duty and prudence, more earnestly to maintain and defend, than the authority of the British parliament to regulate the trade of all her dominions. Without this authority, the benefits she enjoys from our commerce, must be lost to her: The blessings we enjoy from our dependance upon her, must be lost to us; her strength must decay; her glory vanish; and she cannot suffer, without our partaking in her misfortune.——"Let us therefore cherish her interest as our own, and give her every thing that it becomes FREEMEN to give or to receive."

The *nature* of any impositions she may lay upon us, may in general be known, considering how far they relate to the preserving, in due order, the connexion between the[66] several parts of the *British* empire. One thing we may be assured of, which is this; whenever a statute imposes duties on commodities, to be paid only upon their exportation from Great-Britain to these colonies, it is not a regulation of trade, but a design to raise a revenue upon us. Other instances may happen, which it may not be necessary to dwell on. I hope these colonies will never, to their latest existence, want understanding sufficient to discover the intentions of those who rule over them, nor the resolution necessary for asserting their interests. They will always have the same right that all free states have, of judging when their privileges are invaded, and of using all prudent measures for preserving them.

"*Quocirca vivite fortes*"
"*Fortiaque adversis opponite pectora rebus,*"

Wherefore keep up your spirits, and gallantly oppose this adverse course of affairs.

A FARMER.

[67]

LETTER VII.

Beloved Countrymen,

This letter is intended more particularly for such of you, whose employment in life may have prevented your attending to the consideration of some points that are of great and public importance. For many such persons there must be even in these colonies, where the inhabitants in general are more intelligent than any other people, as has been remarked by strangers, and it seems with reason.

Some of you perhaps, filled as I know your breasts are with loyalty to our most excellent prince, and with love to our dear mother country, may feel yourselves inclined by the affections of your hearts, to approve every action of those whom you so much venerate and esteem.

A prejudice thus flowing from goodness of disposition is amiable indeed. I wish it could be indulged without danger. Did I think this possible, the error should have been adopted, not opposed by me. But in truth, all men are subject to the passions and frailties of nature; and therefore whatever regard we entertain for the persons of those who govern us, we should always remember[68] that their conduct as rulers may be influenced by human infirmities.

When any laws injurious to these colonies are passed, we cannot, with the least propriety, suppose that any injury was intended us by his Majesty or the Lords. For the assent of the crown and peers to law seems, as far as I am able to judge, to have been vested in them, more for their own security than for any other purpose. On the other hand, it is the particular business of the people to enquire and discover what regulations are useful for themselves, and to digest and present them in the form of bills to the other orders, to have them enacted into laws—Where these laws are to bind themselves, it may be expected that the house of Commons will very carefully consider them: But when they are making laws, that are not designed to bind themselves, we cannot imagine that their deliberations will be as cautious and scrupulous as in their own case.[31]

I find that this clause "privately got into an act," for the benefit of Capt. Cole, "to the vast loss of the nation," is foisted into the 3d Anne, chap. 5, intituled, "An act for granting to her Majesty a further subsidy on wines and merchandizes imported," with which it has no more connexion, than with 34th Edw. I. 34th and 35th of Henry VIII. or the 25th of Car. II. which provide that no person shall be taxed but by himself or his representative.]

[69]

I am told that there is a wonderful address frequently used in carrying points in the house of commons, by persons experienced in these affairs—that opportunities are watched—and sometimes votes are past, that if all the members had been present, would[70] have been rejected by a great majority. Certain it is, that when a powerful and artful man has determined on any measure against these colonies, he has always succeeded in his attempt. Perhaps therefore it will be proper for us, whenever any oppressive act affecting us is past, to attribute it to the inattention of the members of the house of commons, and to the malevolence or ambition of some factious great man, rather than to any other cause.

Now I do verily believe, that the late act of parliament imposing duties on paper, &c. was formed by Mr. Grenville and his party, because it is evidently a part of that plan, by which he endeavoured to render himself popular at home; and I do also believe that not one half of the members of the house of commons, even of those who heard it read, did perceive how destructive it was to American freedom.

For this reason, as it is usual in Great-Britain, to consider the King's speech, as the speech of the ministry, it may be right here to consider this act as the act of a party.— Perhaps I should speak more properly if I was to use another term.—

[71]

There are two ways of laying taxes.—One is by imposing a certain sum on particular kinds of property, to be paid by the user or consumer, or by taxing the person at a certain sum; the other is, by imposing a certain sum on particular kinds of property to be paid by the seller.

When a man pays the first sort of tax, he knows with certainty that he pays so much money for a tax. The consideration for which he pays it is remote, and it may be does not occur to him. He is sensible too that he is commanded and obliged to pay it as a tax; and therefore people are apt to be displeased with this sort of tax.

The other sort of tax is submitted to in a very different manner. The purchaser of any article very seldom reflects that the seller raises his price so as to indemnify him for the tax he has paid. He knows the prices of things are continually fluctuating, and if he thinks about the tax, he thinks at the same time in all probability, that he might have paid as much, if the article he buys had not been taxed. He gets something visible and agreeable for his money, and tax and price are so confounded together, that he cannot separate, or does not chuse to take the trouble of separating them.

This mode of taxation therefore is the mode suited to arbitrary and oppressive governments. The love of liberty is so natural[72] to the human heart, that unfeeling tyrants think themselves obliged to accommodate their schemes as much as they can to the appearance of justice and reason, and to deceive those whom they resolve to destroy or oppress, by presenting to them a miserable picture of freedom, when the inestimable original is lost.

This policy did not escape the cruel and rapacious Nero. That monster, apprehensive that his crimes might endanger his authority and life, thought proper to do some popular acts to secure the obedience of his subjects. Among other things, says[32] Tacitus, "he remitted the twenty-fifth part of the price on the sale of slaves, but rather in shew than reality; for the seller being ordered to pay it, it became a part of the price to the buyer."

This is the reflection of the judicious historian: but the deluded people gave their infamous emperor full credit for his false generosity. Other nations have been treated in the same manner the Romans were. The honest industrious Germans who are settled in different parts of this continent can inform us, that it was this sort of tax that drove them from their native land to our woods, at that time the seats of perfect and undisturbed freedom.

Their princes inflamed by the lust of power and the lust of avarice, two furies,[73] that the more hungry they grow, transgressed the bounds, they ought in regard to themselves, to have observed. To keep up the deception in the minds of subjects "there must be," says a very learned author[33] "some proportion between the impost and the value of the commodity; wherefore there ought not to be an excessive duty upon merchandizes of little value. There are countries in which the duty exceeds seventeen or eighteen times the value of the commodity. In this case the prince removes the illusion. His subjects plainly see they are dealt with in an unreasonable manner, which renders them most exquisitely sensible of their slavish situation."

From hence it appears that subjects may be ground down into misery by this sort of taxation as well as the other. They may be as much impoverished if their money is taken from them in this way, as in the other; and that it will be taken, may be more evident, by attending to a few more considerations.

The merchant, or importer who pays the duty at first, will not consent to be so much money out of pocket. He, therefore, proportionably raises the price of his goods. It may then be said to be a contest between him and the person offering to buy, who shall lose the duty. This must be decided by the nature of the commodities and the purchasers demand for them. If they are[74] mere luxuries, he is at liberty to do as he pleases, and if he buys, he does it voluntarily: But if they are absolute necessaries, or conveniences which use and custom have made requisite for the comfort of life, and which he is not permitted, by the power imposing the duty, to get elsewhere, there the seller has a plain advantage, and the buyer must pay the duty. In fact, the seller is nothing less than the collector of the tax for the power that imposed it. If these duties then are extended to necessaries and conveniences of life in general, and enormously increased, the people must at length become indeed "most exquisitely sensible of their slavish situation."

Their happiness, therefore, entirely depends on the moderation of those who have authority to impose the duties.

I shall now apply these observations to the late act of parliament. Certain duties are thereby imposed on paper and glass, &c. imported into these colonies. By the laws of *Great-Britain* we are prohibited to get these articles from any other part of the world. We cannot at present, nor for many years to come, though we should apply ourselves to these manufactures with the utmost industry, make enough ourselves for our own use. That paper and glass are not only convenient, but absolutely necessary for us, I imagine very few will contend. Some, perhaps, who think mankind grew wicked and luxurious as soon as they found out another way of communicating[75] their sentiments than by speech, and another way of dwelling than in caves, may advance so whimsical an opinion. But I presume nobody will take the unnecessary trouble of refuting them.

From these remarks I think it evident, that we must use paper and glass, that what we use must be *British*, and that we must pay the duties imposed unless those who sell these articles are so generous as to make us presents of the duties they pay, which is not to be expected.

Some persons may think this act of no consequence, because the duties are so *small*. A fatal error. That is the very circumstance most alarming to me. For I am convinced that the authors of this law, would never have obtained an act to raise so trifling a sum, as it must do, had they not intended by it to establish a *precedent* for future use. To console ourselves with the *smallness* of the duties, is to walk deliberately into the snare that is set for us, praising the *neatness* of the workmanship. Suppose the duties, imposed by the late act, could be paid by these distressed colonies, with the utmost ease, and that the purposes, to which they are to be applied, were the most reasonable and equitable that could be conceived, the contrary of which I hope to demonstrate before these letters are concluded, yet even in such a supposed case, these colonies ought to regard the act with abhorrence. For who are a free people? not those over whom government is reasonably and equitably exercised[76] but those who live under a government, so *constitutionally checked* and *controuled*, that proper provision is made against its being otherwise exercised. The late act is founded on the destruction of this constitutional security.

If the parliament have a right to lay a duty of four shillings and eight pence on a hundred weight of glass, or a ream of paper, they have a right to lay a duty of any other sum on either. They may raise the duty as the author before quoted says, has been done in some countries, till it "exceeds seventeen or eighteen times the value of the commodity." In short, if they have a right to levy a tax of *one penny* upon us, they have a right to levy a *million* upon us. For where does their right stop? At any given number of pence, shillings, or pounds? To attempt to limit their right, after granting it to exist at all, is as contrary to reason, as granting it to exist at all is contrary to justice. If they have any right to tax us, then, whether our own money shall continue in our own pockets, or not, depends no longer on *us*, but on *them*. "There is nothing which we can call our own", or to use the words of Mr. *Locke*, "What property have" we "in that, which another may, by right, take, when he pleases, to himself."[34]

These duties, which will inevitably be levied upon us, and which are now levying upon us, are expressly laid for the sole purpose of taking money. This is the true definition[77] of taxes. They are therefore taxes. This money is to be taken from us. We are therefore taxed. Those who are taxed without their own consent, given by themselves, or their representatives, are slaves.[35] We are[78] taxed without our own consent given by ourselves, or our representatives. We are therefore——I speak it with grief——I speak it with indignation——we are slaves.

"*Miserabile vulgus.*"
A miserable tribe.

A FARMER.

[79]

LETTER VIII.

Beloved Countrymen,

In my opinion, a dangerous example is set in the last act relating to these colonies. The power of parliament to levy money upon us for raising a revenue, is therein avowed and exerted. Regarding the act on this single principle, I must again repeat, and I think it my duty to repeat, that to me it appears to be unconstitutional.

No man, who considers the conduct of parliament since the repeal of the Stamp-act, and the disposition of many people at home, can doubt, that the chief object of attention there, is, to use Mr. Grenville's expression, "providing that the dependance and obedience of the colonies be asserted and maintained."

Under the influence of this notion, instantly on repealing the Stamp-act, an act passed, declaring the power of parliament to bind these colonies in all cases whatever. This, however, was only planting a barren tree, that cast a shade indeed over the colonies, but yielded no fruit. It being determined to enforce the authority on which the Stamp-act was founded, the parliament having never renounced the right, as Mr. Pitt advised them to do; and it being thought[80] proper to disguise that authority in such a manner, as not again to alarm the colonies; some little time was required to find a method, by which both these points should be united. At last the ingenuity of Mr. Greenville and his party accomplished the matter, as it was thought, in "An act for granting certain duties in the British colonies and plantations in America, for allowing drawbacks, &c. which is the title of the act laying duties on paper, &c."

34

The parliament having several times before imposed duties to be paid in America, it was expected no doubt, that the repetition of such a measure would be passed over as an usual thing. But to have done this, without expressly asserting and maintaining "the power of parliament to take our money without our consent," and to apply it as they please, would not have been sufficiently declarative of its supremacy, nor sufficiently depressive of American freedom.

Therefore it is, that in this memorable act we find it expressly "provided" that money shall be levied upon us without our consent, for purposes, that render it, if possible, more dreadful than the Stamp-act.

That act, alarming as it was, declared, the money thereby to be raised, should be applied "towards defraying the expences of defending, protecting and securing the British colonies and plantations in America:" And it is evident from the whole act, that by the word "British" were intended[81] colonies and plantations settled by British people, and not generally, those subject to the British crown. That act therefore seemed to have something gentle and kind in its intention, and to aim only at our own welfare: But the act now objected to, imposes duties upon the British colonies, "to defray the expences of defending, protecting and securing his Majesty's dominions in America."

What a change of words! What an incomputable addition to the expences intended by the Stamp-act! "His Majesty's dominions" comprehended not only the British colonies; but also the conquered provinces of Canada and Florida, and the British garrisons of Nova-Scotia; for these do not deserve the name of colonies.

What justice is there in making us pay for "defending, protecting and securing" these places? What benefit can we, or have we ever derived from them? None of them was conquered for us; nor will "be defended, protected and secured" for us.

In fact, however advantageous the subduing or keeping any of these countries may be to Great-Britain, the acquisition is greatly injurious to these colonies. Our chief property consists in lands. These would have been of a much greater value, if such prodigious additions had not been made to the British territories on this continent. The natural increase of our own people, if confined within[82] the colonies, would have raised the value still higher and higher, every fifteen or twenty years. Besides, we should have lived more compactly together, and have been therefore more able to resist any enemy.

But now the inhabitants will be thinly scattered over an immense region, as those who want settlements, will chuse to make new ones, rather than pay great prices for old ones.

These are the consequences to the colonies of the hearty assistance they gave to Great-Britain in the late war.——A war, undertaken solely for her own benefit. The objects of it were, the securing to herself the rich tracts of land on the back of these colonies, with the Indian trade, and Nova-Scotia with the fishery. These, and much more has that kingdom gained; but the inferior animals that hunted with the Lion, have been amply rewarded for all the sweat and blood their loyalty cost them, by the honour of having sweated and bled in such company.

I will not go so far as to say, that Canada and Nova-Scotia are curbs on New-England; the chain of forts through the back woods, on the middle provinces; and Florida, on the rest: but I will venture to say, that if the products of Canada, Nova-Scotia and Florida, deserve any consideration, the two first of them are only rivals of our northern colonies and the other of our southern.

[83]

It has been said, that without the conquest of these countries, the colonies could not have been "protected, defended, and secured;" If that is true, it may with as much propriety be said, that Great-Britain could not have been "defended, protected, and secured" without that conquest: for the colonies are parts of her empire, which it is as much concerns her as them to keep out of the hands of any other power.

But these colonies when they were much weaker, defended themselves, before this conquest was made; and could again do it, against any that might properly be called their enemies. If France and Spain indeed should attack them, as members of the British empire perhaps they might be distressed; but it would be in a British quarrel.

The largest account I have seen of the number of people in Canada, does not make them exceed 90,000. Florida can hardly be said to have any inhabitants——It is computed that there are in our colonies, 3,000,000.—Our force therefore must encrease with a disproportion to the growth of their strength, that would render us very safe.

This being the state of the case, I cannot think it just, that these colonies, labouring under so many misfortunes, should be loaded with taxes, to maintain countries not only not useful, but hurtful to them. The support of Canada and Florida cost yearly, it is said, half a million sterling. From hence we[84] may make some guess of the load that is to be laid upon us; for we are not only to "defend, protect, and secure" them, but also to make "an adequate provision for defraying the charge of the administration of justice and the support of civil government, in such provinces where it shall be found necessary."

Not one of the provinces of Canada, Nova-Scotia, or Florida, has ever defrayed these expences within itself: And if the duties imposed by the last statute are collected, all of them together, according to the best information I can get, will not pay one-quarter as much as Pennsylvania alone. So that the British colonies are to be drained of the rewards of their labour, to cherish the scorching sands of Florida, and the icy rocks of Canada and Nova-Scotia, which never will return to us one farthing that we send to them.

Great-Britain——I mean the ministry in Great-Britain, has cantoned Canada and Florida out into five or six governments, and may form as many more. She now has fourteen or fifteen regiments on this continent; and may send over as many more. To make "an adequate provision" for all these expences, is, no doubt, to be the inheritance of the colonies.

Can any man believe that the duties upon paper, &c. are the last that will be laid for these purposes? It is in vain to hope, that because it is imprudent to lay duties on the[85]exportation of manufactures from a mother country to colonies, as it may promote manufactures among them, that this consideration will prevent them.

Ambitious, artful men have made the measure popular, and whatever injustice or destruction will attend it in the opinion of the colonists, at home it will be thought just and salutary.[36]

The people of Great-Britain will be told, and they have been told, that they are sinking under an immense debt—that great part of this debt has been contracted in defending the colonies—that these are so ungrateful and undutiful, that they will not contribute one mite to its payment—nor even to the support of the army now kept up for their "protection and security"—that they are rolling in wealth, and are of so bold and republican a spirit, that they are aiming at independence—that the only way to retain them in "obedience" is to keep a strict watch over them, and to draw off part of their riches in taxes—and that every burden laid upon them is taking off so much from Great-Britain—These assertions will be generally believed, and the people will be persuaded that they cannot be too angry with their colonies, as that anger will be profitable to themselves.

[86]
In truth, Great-Britain alone receives any benefit from Canada, Nova-Scotia, and Florida; and therefore she alone ought to maintain them.—The old maxim of the law is drawn from reason and justice, and never could be more properly applied, than in this case.

"Qui sentit, commodum, sentire debet et onus."
They who feel the benefit, ought to feel the burden.

A FARMER.

[87]

LETTER IX.

Beloved Countrymen,
I have made some observations on the purposes for which money is to be levied upon us by the late act of parliament. I shall now offer to your consideration some further reflections on that subject; and, unless I am greatly mistaken, if these purposes are accomplished, according to the exprest intention of the act, they will be found effectually to supersede that authority in our respective assemblies, which is most essential to liberty. The

question is not whether some branches shall be lopt off—The ax is laid to the root of the tree; and the whole body must infallibly perish, if we remain idle spectators of the work.

No free people ever existed, or ever can exist, without, keeping, to use a common but strong expression, "the purse strings" in their own hands. Where this is the case, they have a constitutional check upon the administration, which may thereby be brought into order without violence: but where such a power is not lodged in the people, oppression proceeds uncontrouled in its career, till the governed, transported[88] into rage, seeks redress in the midst of blood and confusion.

The elegant and ingenious Mr. Hume, speaking of the Anglo-Norman government, says "princes and ministers were too ignorant to be themselves sensible of the advantages attending an equitable administration; and there was no established council or assembly which could protect the people, and, by withdrawing supplies, regularly and peaceably admonish the King of his duty, and ensure the execution of the laws."

Thus this great man, whose political reflections are so much admired, makes this power one of the foundations of liberty.

The English history abounds with instances, proving that this is the proper and successful way to obtain redress of grievances. How often have Kings and ministers endeavoured to throw off this legal curb upon them, by attempting to raise money by a variety of inventions, under pretence of law, without having recourse to parliament? And how often have they been brought to reason, and peaceably obliged to do justice, by the exertion of this constitutional authority of the people, vested in their representatives?

The inhabitants of these colonies have on numberless occasions, reaped the benefits of this authority lodged in their assemblies.

[89]

It has been for a long time, and now is, a constant instruction to all governors, to obtain a permanent support for the officers of government. But as the author of the administration of the colonies says, "this order of the crown is generally, if not universally, rejected by the legislatures of the colonies."

They perfectly know how much their grievances would be regarded, if they had no other method of engaging attention, than by complaining. Those who rule, are extremely apt to think well of the constructions made by themselves, in support of their own power. These are frequently erroneous and pernicious to those they govern—Dry remonstrances, to shew that such constructions are wrong and oppressive, carry very little weight with them, in the opinion of persons, who gratify their own inclinations in making these constructions. They cannot understand the reasoning that opposes their power and desire: but let it be made their interest to understand such reasoning—and a wonderful light is instantly thrown on the matter; and then rejected remonstrances become as clear as "proof of holy writ."[37]

The three most important articles, that our assemblies, or any legislatures can provide for, are, first the defence of the society:[90] secondly—the administration of justice: and, thirdly, the support of civil government.

Nothing can properly regulate the expence of making provision for these occasions, but the necessities of the society; its abilities; the conveniency of the modes of levying money among them; the manner in which the laws have been executed; and the conduct of the officers of government; all which are circumstances that cannot possibly be properly known, but by the society itself; or, if they should be known, will not, probably, be properly considered, but by that society.

If money may be raised upon us, by others, without our consent, for our "defence," those who are the judges in levying it, must also be the judges in applying it. Of consequence, the money said to be taken from us for our defence, may be employed to our injury. We may be chained in by a line of fortifications: obliged to pay for building and maintaining them; and be told that they are for our defence. With what face can we dispute the fact, after having granted, that those who apply the money, had a right to levy it; for, surely, it is much easier for their wisdom to understand how to apply it in the best manner, than how to levy it in the best manner. Besides, the right of levying is of infinitely more consequence, than that of applying it. The people of England, that would burst out into[91] fury, if the crown should attempt to levy money by its own authority, have assigned to the crown the application of money.

As to "the administration of justice"—the judges ought, in a well regulated state, to be equally independant of the legislative powers. Thus, in England, judges hold their commissions from the crown "during good behaviour;" and have salaries, suitable to their dignity, settled on them by parliament. The purity of the courts of law, since this establishment, is a proof of the wisdom with which it was made.

But, in these colonies, how fruitless has been every attempt to have the judges appointed during good behaviour; yet whoever considers the matter will soon perceive, that such commissions are beyond all comparison more necessary in these colonies, than they are in England.

The chief danger to the subject there, arose from the arbitrary designs of the crown; but here, the time may come, when we may have to contend with the designs of the crown, and of a mighty kingdom. What then will be our chance, when the laws of life and death, are to be spoken by judges, totally dependant on that crown and kingdom—sent over, perhaps, from thence—filled with British prejudice—and backed by a standing army, supported out of our own pockets, to "assert and maintain" our own "dependance and obedience."

[92]

But supposing, that through the extreme lenity that will prevail in the government, through all future ages, these colonies never will behold any thing like the campaign of chief justice Jeffereys, yet what innumerable acts of injustice may be committed, and how fatally may the principles of liberty be sapped by a succession of judges utterly independant of the people? Before such judges, the supple wretches, who cheerfully join in avowing sentiments inconsistent with freedom, will always meet with smiles: while the honest and brave men, who disdain to sacrifice their native land to their own advantage, but on every occasion, boldly vindicate her cause, will constantly be regarded with frowns.

There are two other considerations, relating to this head, that deserve the most serious attention.

By the late act the officers of the customs are impowered "to enter into any house, warehouse, shop, cellar, or other place, in the British colonies or plantations in America, to search for, or seize prohibited or unaccustomed goods," &c. on "writs granted by the inferior or supreme court of justice, having jurisdiction within such colony or plantation respectively."

If we only reflect that the judges of these courts are to be *during pleasure*—that they are to have "*adequate provision*" made for them, which is to continue during their*complisant behaviour*—that they may be[93] stranger to these colonies—what an engine of oppression may this authority be in such hands?

I am well aware that writs of this kind may be granted at home, under the seal of the court of exchequer: But I know also that the greatest asserters of the rights of Englishmen, have always strenuously contended, that such a power was dangerous to freedom, and expressly contrary to the common law, which ever regarded a man's house, as his castle, or a place of perfect security.

If such a power is in the least degree dangerous there, it must be utterly destructive to liberty here.—For the people there have two securities against the undue exercise of this power by the crown, which are wanting with us, if the late act takes place. In the first place, if any injustice is done there, the person injured may bring his action against the offender, and have it tried by independant judges, who are[38] no parties in committing the injury. Here he must have it tried before dependant judges, being the men who granted the writ.

To say that the cause is to be tried by a jury can never reconcile men, who have any idea of freedom to such a power.—For we know, that sheriffs in almost every colony[94] on this continent, are totally dependant on the crown; and packing of juries has been frequently practiced even in the capital of the British empire. Even if juries are well inclined, we have too many instances of the influence of overbearing unjust judges upon them. The brave and wise men who accomplished the revolution, thought the independency of judges essential to freedom.

The other security which the people have at home, but which we shall want here, is this.—If this power is abused there, the parliament, the grand resource of the opprest people, is ready to afford relief. Redress of grievances must precede grants of money. But what regard can we expect to be paid to our assemblies, when they will not hold even the puny privilege of French parliaments——that of registering the edicts, that take away our money, before they are put in execution.

The second consideration above hinted at, is this—There is a confusion in our laws that is quite unknown in Great-Britain. As this cannot be described in a more clear or exact manner, than has been done by the ingenious author of the history of New-York, I beg leave to use his words. "The state of our laws opens a door to much controversy. The uncertainty which respect them, renders property precarious, and greatly exposes us to the arbitrary decision of unjust judges.[95] The common law of England is generally received, together with such statutes, as were enacted before we had a legislature of our own; but our courts exercise a sovereign authority, in determining what parts of the common and statute law ought to be extended: For it must be admitted, that the difference of circumstances necessarily requires us, in some cases, to reject the determination of both. In many instances they have also extended even acts of parliament, passed since we had a distinct legislature, which is greatly adding to our confusion. The practice of our courts is no less uncertain than the law. Some of the English rules are adopted, others rejected. Two things therefore seem to be absolutely necessary for the public security. First the passing an act for settling the extent of the English laws. Secondly, that the courts ordain a general set of rules for the regulation of the practice."

How easy will it be under this "state of our laws" for an artful judge to act in the most arbitrary manner, and yet cover his conduct under specious pretences, and how difficult will it be for the injured people to obtain redress, may be readily perceived. We may take a voyage of three thousand miles to complain; and after the trouble and hazard we have undergone, we may be told, that the collection of the revenue and maintenance of the prerogative, must not be discouraged.——And if the misbehaviour is so[96] gross as to admit of no justification, it may be said that it was an error in judgment only, arising from the confusion of our laws, and the zeal of the King's servants to do their duty.

If the commissions of judges are during the pleasure of the crown, yet if their salaries are during the pleasure of the people, there will be some check upon their conduct. Few men will consent to draw on themselves the hatred and contempt of those among whom we live, for the empty honour of being judges. It is the sordid love of gain that tempts men to turn their backs on virtue, and pay their homage where they ought not.

As to the third particular, the "support of civil government," few words will be sufficient. Every man of the least understanding must know, that the executive power may be exercised in a manner so disagreeable and harassing to the people, that it is absolutely requisite, they should be enabled by the gentlest method which human policy has yet been ingenious enough to invent, that is by the shutting their hands, to "admonish" (as Mr. Hume says) certain persons "of their duty."

What shall we now think, when, upon looking into the late act, we find the assemblies of these provinces thereby stript of their authority on these several heads? The declared intention of that act is, "that a revenue[97] should be raised in his Majesty's dominions in America, for making a more certain and adequate provision for defraying the charge of the administration of justice, and the support of civil government, in such provinces where it shall be found necessary; and towards further defraying the expences of defending, protecting, and securing the said dominions," &c.

Let the reader pause here one moment, and reflect—whether the colony in which he lives, has not made such "certain and adequate provisions" for these purposes, as is by the colony judged suitable to its abilities, and all other circumstances. Then let him reflect— whether, if this act takes place, money is not to be raised on that colony without its consent to make provision for these purposes, which it does not judge to be suitable to its abilities, and all other circumstances. Lastly, let him reflect—whether the people of that country are not in a state of the most abject slavery, whose property may be taken from them under the notion of right, when they have refused to give it. For my part, I think I have good reason for vindicating the honour of the assemblies on this continent, by publicly asserting, that they have made as "certain and adequate provision" for the purposes above-mentioned, as they ought to have made; and that it should not be presumed, that they will not do it hereafter. Why then[98] should these most important truths be wrested out of their hands? Why should they not now be permitted to enjoy that authority, which they have exercised from the first settlement of these colonies? Why should they be scandalized by this innovation, when their respective provinces are now, and will be for several years, labouring under loads of debts imposed on them for the very purposes now spoken of? Why should the inhabitants of all these colonies be with the utmost indignity treated, as a herd of despicable wretches, so utterly void of common sense, that they will not even make "adequate provision" for the "administration of justice" and "the support of civil government" among them, for their "own defence"—though without such "provision" every people must inevitably be overwhelmed with anarchy and destruction? Is it possible to form an idea of slavery more complete, more miserable, more disgraceful, than that of a people, where justice is administered, government exercised, and a standing army maintained, at the expence of the people, and yet without the least dependance upon them? If we can find no relief from this infamous situation, let Mr. Grenville set his fertile fancy again to work, and as by one exertion of it, he has stripped us of our property and liberty, let him by another deprive us of our understanding too, that unconscious of what we have[99] been or are, and ungoaded by tormenting reflections, we may tamely bow down our necks with all the stupid serenity of servitude, to any drudgery, which our lords and masters may please to command.—

When the "charges of the administration of justice,"—"the support of civil government;"—and "the expences of defending protecting and securing" us, are provided for, I should be glad to know upon what occasion the crown will ever call our assemblies together. Some few of them may meet of their own accord, by virtue of their charters: But what will they have to do when they are met? To what shadows will they be reduced? The men, whose deliberations heretofore had an influence on every matter relating to the liberty and happiness of themselves and their constituents, and whose authority in domestic affairs, at least, might well be compared to that of Roman senators, will now find their deliberations of no more consequence than those of constables.—They may perhaps be allowed to make laws for yoking of hogs, or pounding of stray cattle. Their influence will hardly be permitted to extend so high as the keeping roads in repair, as that business may more properly be executed by those who receive the public cash.

One most memorable example in history is so applicable to the point now insisted on,[100] that it will form a just conclusion of the observations that have been made.

Spain was once free. Their *Cortes* resembled our parliament. No money could be raised on the subject, without their consent. One of their Kings having received a grant from them to maintain a war against the Moors, desired, that if the sum which they had given, should not be sufficient, he might be allowed for that emergency only, to have more money, without assembling the *Cortes*. The request was violently opposed by the best and wisest men in the assembly. It was however, complied with by the votes of a majority; and this single concession was a precedent for other concessions of the like kinds, until, at last, the crown obtained a general power for raising money in cases of necessity. From that period the *Cortes* ceased to be useful, and the people ceased to be free.

Venienti occurrite morbo.
Oppose a disease at its beginning.—

A FARMER.

[101]

LETTER X.

Beloved Countrymen,

The consequences, mentioned in the last letter, will not be the utmost limits of our misery and infamy. We feel too sensibly that any[32] ministerial measures, relating to these colonies, are soon carried successfully thro' the parliament. Certain prejudices operate there so strongly against us, that it might justly be questioned, whether all the provinces united, will ever be able effectually to call to an account, before the parliament, any minister who shall abuse the power by the late act given to the crown in America. He may divide the spoils torn from us, in what manner he pleases; and we shall have no way of making him responsible. If he should order, that every Governor, should have a yearly salary of 5000*l.* sterling, every chief justice of 3000*l.* every inferior officer[102] in proportion; and should then reward the most profligate, ignorant, or needy dependants on himself, or his friends with places of the greatest trust because they were of the greatest profit, this would be called an arrangement in consequence of the "adequate provision for defraying the charge of the administration of justice, and the support of the civil government." And if the taxes should prove at any time insufficient to answer all the expences of the numberless offices, which ministers may please to create, surely the house of Commons would be too "modest" to contradict a minister who should tell them, it was become necessary to lay a new tax upon the colonies, for the laudable purpose of "defraying the charges of the administration of justice, and the support of civil government" among them. Thus in fact we shall be taxed by ministers.[40]

We may perceive, from the example of Ireland, how eager ministers are to seize upon any settled revenue, and apply it in supporting their own power.———Happy are the men, and happy are the people, who grow wise by the misfortune of others. Earnestly, my dear countrymen, do I beseech the author of all good gifts, that you may grow wise in this manner: And, if I may be allowed[103] to take the liberty, I beg leave to recommend to you in general, as the best method of obtaining wisdom, diligently to study the histories of other countries. You will there find all the arts, that can possibly be practiced by cunning rulers, or false patriots among yourselves, so fully delineated, that changing names, the account would serve for your own times.

It is pretty well known on this continent, that Ireland has, with a regular consistence of injustice, been cruelly treated by ministers in the article of pensions; but there are some alarming circumstances relating to that subject, which I wish to have better known among us. [41] The revenue of the crown there, arises principally from the excise granted "for pay of the army, and defraying other public charges in defence and preservation of the kingdom"— from the tonnage and additional poundage granted "for protecting the trade of the kingdom at sea, and augmenting the public revenue" from the hearth-money granted, as a "public revenue for public charges and expences." There are some other branches of the revenue, concerning which there is not any express appropriation of them for public service, but which were plainly so intended.

[104]

Of these branches of the revenue, the crown is only a trustee for the public. They are unalienable; they are inapplicable to any other purposes, but those for which they were established; and therefore are not legally chargeable with pensions.

There is another kind of revenue, which is a private revenue. This is not limited to any public uses; but the crown has the same property in it, that any person has in his estate. This does not amount at the most to fifteen thousand pounds a year, probably not to seven; and it is the only revenue that can legally be charged with pensions. If ministers were accustomed to regard the rights or happiness of the people, the pensions in Ireland would not exceed the sum just mentioned: but long since have they exceeded that limit, and in December, 1765, a motion was made in the House of Commons in that kingdom, to address his Majesty, on the great increase of pensions on the Irish establishment, amounting to the sum of £.158,685 in the last two years.

Attempts have been made to gloss over these gross incroachments, by this specious argument,—"That expending a competent part of the public revenue in pensions, from a principle of charity or generosity, adds to the dignity of the crown, and is, therefore, useful to the public." To give this argument any weight, it must appear that the pensions proceed from "charity[105] or generosity" only—And that it "adds to the dignity of the crown" to act directly contrary to law.

From this conduct towards Ireland, in open violation of law, we may easily foresee what we may expect, when a minister will have the whole revenue of America, in his own hands, to be disposed of at his own pleasure. For all the monies raised by the late act are to be "applied, by virtue of warrants under the sign manual, countersigned by the high treasurer, or any three of the commissioners of the treasury." The "residue" indeed, is to be paid "into the receipt of the exchequer, and to be disposed of by parliament." So that a minister will have nothing to do but to take care that there shall be no "residue," and he is superior to all controul.

Besides the burden of pensions in Ireland, which have enormously encreased within these few years, almost all the offices, in that poor kingdom, have, since the commencement of the present century, and now are bestowed upon strangers. For though the merit of those born there justly raises them to places of high trust, when they go abroad, as all Europe can witness, yet he is an uncommonly lucky Irishman, who can get a good post in his native country.

[106]

When I consider the[42]manner in which that island has been uniformly depressed for so many years past, with this pernicious particularity[107] of their parliament continuing[43] as long as the crown pleases, I am astonished to observe such a love of liberty still animating that loyal and generous nation; and nothing can raise higher my idea of the integrity and public spirit of the people[108][44] who have preserved the sacred fire of freedom from being extinguished though the altar, on which it burned, has been thrown down.

In the same manner shall we unquestionably be treated, as soon as the late taxes, laid upon us, shall make posts in the "government," and the "administration of justice," here, worth the attention of persons of influence in Great Britain. We know enough already to satisfy us of this truth. But this will not be the worst part of our case.

The principals in all great offices will reside in England, make some paltry allowance to deputies for doing the business here. Let any man consider what an exhausting drain this must be upon us, when ministers are possessed of the power of affixing what[109]salaries they please to posts, and he must be convinced how destructive the late act must be. The injured kingdom, lately mentioned, can tell us the mischiefs of absentees; and we may perceive already the same disposition taking place with us. The government of New York has been exercised by a deputy. That of Virginia is now held so; and we know of a number of secretaryships, collectorships, and other offices held in the same manner.

True it is, that if the people of Great-Britain were not too much blinded by the passions, that have been artfully excited in their breasts, against their dutiful children, the colonists, these considerations would be nearly as alarming to them as to us. The influence of the crown was thought, by wise men many years ago, too great, by reason of the multitude of pensions and places bestowed by it; these have vastly increased since[45] and perhaps it would be no difficult[110] matter to prove that the people have decreased.

Surely, therefore, those who wish the welfare of their country, ought seriously to reflect what may be the consequence of such a new creation of offices, in the disposal of the crown. The army, the administration of justice, and the civil government here, with such salaries as the crown shall please to annex, will extend ministerial influence, as much beyond its former bounds, as the late war did the British dominions.

But whatever the people of Great-Britain may think on this occasion, I hope the people of these colonies will unanimously join in this sentiment, that the late act of parliament is injurious to their liberty; and that this sentiment will unite them in a firm opposition[111] to it, in the same manner as the dread of the Stamp-act did.

Some persons may imagine the sums to be raised by it, are but small, and therefore may be inclined to acquiesce under it. A conduct more dangerous to freedom, as before has been observed, can never be adopted. Nothing is wanted at home but a precedent, the force of which shall be established, by the tacit submission of the colonies. With what zeal was the statute erecting the post-office, and another relating to the recovery of debts in America, urged and tortured, as precedents in the support of the Stamp-act, though wholly inapplicable. If the parliament succeeds in this attempt, other statutes will impose other duties. Instead of taxing ourselves as we have been accustomed to do from the first settlement of these provinces; all our useful taxes will be converted into parliamentary taxes on our importations; and thus the parliament will levy upon us such sums of money as they chuse to take, without any other limitation than their pleasure.

We know how much labour and care have been bestowed by these colonies, in laying taxes in such a manner, that they should be most easy to the people, by being laid on the proper articles; most equal, by being proportioned to every man's circumstances; and cheapest by the method directed for collecting them.

[112]

But parliamentary taxes will be laid on us without any consideration, whether there is any eassier mode. The only point regarded will be, the certainty of levying the taxes, and not the convenience of the people, on whom they are to be levied, and therefore all statutes on this head will be such as will be most likely, according to the favourite phrase, "to execute themselves."

Taxes in every free state have been, and ought to be as exactly proportioned, as is possible, to the abilities of those who are to pay them. They cannot otherwise be just. Even a Hottentot could comprehend the unreasonableness, of making a poor man pay as much for defending the property of a rich man, as the rich man pays himself.

Let any person look into the late act of parliament, and he will immediately perceive, that the immense estates of Lord Fairfax, Lord Baltimore,[46] and our proprietors, which are amongst "his Majesty's other dominions" to be "defended, protected and secured" by that act will not pay a single farthing of the duties thereby imposed, except Lord Fairfax wants some of his windows glazed. Lord Baltimore, and our proprietors[113] are quite secure, as they live in England.

I mention these particular cases as striking instances, how far the late act is a deviation from that principle of justice, which has so constantly distinguished our own laws on this continent.

The third consideration with our continental assemblies in laying taxes has been the method of collecting them. This has been done by a few officers under the inspection of the respective assemblies, with moderate allowances. No more was raised from the subject, than was used for the intended purposes. But by the late act, a minister may appoint as many officers as he pleases for collecting the taxes; may assign them what salaries he thinks "adequate" and they are to be subject to no inspection but his own.

In short, if the late act of parliament takes effect, these colonies must dwindle down into "common corporations," as their enemies in the debates concerning the repeal of the Stamp-act, strenuously insisted they were: and it is not improbable, that some future historians will thus record our fall.

"The eighth year of this reign was distinguished by a very memorable event, the American colonies then submitting for the first time, to be taxed by the British parliament. An attempt of this kind had been made two years before, but was defeated by[114] the vigorous exertions of the several provinces in defence of their liberties. Their behaviour on that occasion rendered their name very celebrated for a short time all over Europe; all states being extremely attentive to a dispute between Great-Britain and so considerable a part of her dominions. For as she was thought to be grown too powerful by the successful conclusion of the late war she had been engaged in, it was hoped by many, that as it had happened before to other kingdoms, civil discords would afford opportunities of revenging all the injuries supposed to be received from her. However the cause of dissention was removed by a repeal of the statute, that had given offense. This affair rendered the submissive conduct of the colonies so soon after, the more extraordinary; there being no difference between the modes of taxation which they opposed, and that to which they submitted, but this, that by the first, they were to be continually reminded that they were taxed, by certain marks stampt on every piece of paper or parchment, they used. The authors of that statute triumphed greatly on this conduct of the colonies, and insisted that if the people of Great-Britain, had persisted in enforcing it, the Americans would have been in a few months so fatigued with the efforts of patriotism, that they would quickly have yielded obedience.

[115]

"Certain it is, that though they had before their eyes so many illustrious examples in their mother country, of the constant success attending firmness and perseverance in opposition to dangerous encroachments on liberty, yet they quietly gave up a point of the last importance. From thence the decline of their freedom began, and its decay was extremely rapid; for as money was always raised upon them by the parliament, their assemblies grew immediately useless and in a short time contemptible; and in less than one hundred years, the people sunk down into that tameness and supineness of spirit by which they still continue to be distinguished."

Et majores vestros et posteros cogitate.

Remember your ancestors and your posterity.

A FARMER.

[116]

[117]

LETTER XI.

Beloved Countrymen,

I have several times, in the course of these letters, mentioned the late act of parliament, as being the foundation of future measures injurious to these colonies; and the belief of this truth I wish to prevail, because I think it necessary to our safety.

A perpetual jealousy respecting liberty, is absolutely requisite in all free states. The very texture of their constitution, in mixt governments, demands it. For the cautions with which power is distributed among the several orders, imply, that each has that share which is proper for the general welfare, and therefore, that any further imposition mull be pernicious.[47]Machiavel employs a whole chapter in his discourses, to prove that a state, to be long lived, must be frequently corrected, and reduced to its first principles. But of all states that have existed, there never was any, in which this jealousy could be more proper than in these colonies. For the government here is not only mixt, but dependant, which circumstance[118] occasions a peculiarity in its form, of a very delicate nature.

Two reasons induce me to desire, that this spirit of apprehension may be always kept up among us, in its utmost vigilance. The first is this, that as the happiness of these provinces indubitably consists in their connection with Great-Britain, any separation between them is less likely to be occasioned by civil discords, if every disgusting measure is opposed singly, and while it is new: for in this manner of proceeding, every such measure is most likely to be rectified. On the other hand, oppressions and dissatisfactions being permitted to accumulate—if ever the governed throw off the load, they will do more. A people does not reform with moderation. The rights of the subject therefore cannot be too often considered, explained, or asserted: and whoever attempts to do this, shews himself, whatever may be the rash and peevish reflections of pretended wisdom, and pretended duty, a friend to those who injudiciously exercise their power, as well as to them, over whom it is so exercised.

Had all the points of prerogative claimed by Charles I. been separately contested and settled in preceding reigns, his fate would in all probability have been very different, and the people would have been content with that liberty which is compatible with regal[119]authority. But[48] he thought, it would be as dangerous for him to give up the powers which at any time had been by usurpation exercised by the crown, as those that were legally vested in it. This produced an equal excess on the part of the people. For when their passions were excited by multiplied grievances, they thought it would be as dangerous for them, to allow the powers that were legally vested in the crown, as those which at any time had been by usurpation exercised by it. Acts, that might by themselves have been upon many considerations excused or extenuated, derived a contagious malignancy and odium from other acts, with which they were connected. They were not regarded according to the simple force of each, but as parts of a system of oppression. Every one therefore, however small in itself, being alarming, as an additional evidence of tyrannical designs. It was in vain for prudent and moderate men to insist, that there was no necessity to abolish royalty. Nothing less than the utter[120]destruction of monarchy, could satisfy those who had suffered, and thought they had reason to believe, they always should suffer under it.

The consequences of these mutual distrusts are well known: But there is no other people mentioned in history, that I recollect, who have been so constantly watchful of their liberty, and so successful in their struggles for it, as the English. This consideration leads me

44

to the second reason, why I "desire that the spirit of apprehension may be always kept up among us in its utmost vigilance."

The first principles of government are to be looked for in human nature. Some of the best writers have asserted, and it seems with good reason, that "government is founded on[49]opinion."

Custom undoubtedly has a mighty force in producing opinion, and reigns in nothing[121]more arbitrarily than in public affairs. It gradually reconciles us to objects even of dread and detestation; and I cannot but think these lines of Mr. Pope, as applicable to vice in politics, as to vice in ethics.

'Vice is a monster of so horrid mien,
As to be hated, needs but to be seen;
Yet seen too oft, familiar with her face,
We first endure, then pity, then embrace.'

When an act injurious to freedom has been once done, and the people bear it, the repetition of it is most likely to meet with submission. For as the mischief of the one was found to be tolerable, they will hope that of the second will prove so too; and they will not regard the infamy of the last, because they are stained with that of the first.

Indeed, nations in general, are not apt to think until they feel; and therefore nations in general have lost their liberty: For as violations of the rights of the governed, are commonly not only specious,[50] but small at the beginning, they spread over the multitude in such a manner, as to touch individuals but slightly. Thus they are disregarded.[51] The power or profit that arises[122] from these violations, centering in few persons, is to them considerable. For this reason the governors having in view their particular purposes, successively preserve an uniformity of conduct for attaining them. They regularly increase and multiply the first injuries, till at length the inattentive people are compelled to perceive the heaviness of their burdens.—They begin to complain and enquire—but too late.—They find their oppressors so strengthened by success, and themselves so entangled in examples of express authority on the part of their rulers, and of tacit recognition on their own part, that they are quite confounded: For millions entertain no other idea of the legality of power, than that it is founded on the exercise of power. They voluntarily fatten their chains, by adopting a pusillanimous opinion, "that there will be too much danger in attempting a remedy," or another opinion no less fatal, "that the government has a right to treat them as it does."[123] They then seek a wretched relief for their minds, by persuading themselves, that to yield their obedience is to discharge their duty. The deplorable poverty of spirit, that prostrates all the dignity bestowed by divine providence on our nature—of course succeeds.

From these reflections I conclude, that every free State should incessantly watch, and instantly take alarm on any condition being made to the power exercised over them, innumerable instances might be produced to shew, from what slight beginnings the most extensive consequences have flowed: but I shall select two only from the history of England.

Henry the seventh was the first monarch of that kingdom, who established a standing body of armed men. This was a band of 50 archers, called yeomen of the guard: And this institution, notwithstanding the smallness of the number, was, to prevent discontent,[52]"disguised under the pretence of majesty and grandeur." In 1684, the standing forces were so much augmented, that Rapin says—"The King, in order to make his people fully sensible of their new slavery, affected to muster his troops, which amounted to 4000 well armed and disciplined men." I think our army, at this time, consists of more than seventy regiments.

[124]
The method of taxing by excise was first introduced amidst the convulsions of civil wars. Extreme necessity was pretended, and its short continuance promised. After the restoration, an excise upon beer, ale and other liquors, was granted to the[53] King, one half in fee, the other for life, as an equivalent for the court of wards. Upon James the second's accession, the parliament[54] gave him the first excise, with an additional duty on wine, tobacco, and some other things. Since the revolution it has been extended to salt, candles, leather, hides, hops, soap, paper, paste-board, mill-boards, scaleboards, vellum, parchment,

starch, silks, calicoes, linens, stuffs, printed, stained, &c. wire, wrought plate, coffee, tea, chocolate, &c.

Thus a standing army and excise have, from the first slender origins, tho' always hated, always feared, always opposed, at length swelled up to their vast present bulk.

These facts are sufficient to support what I have said. 'Tis true that all the mischiefs apprehended by our ancestors from a standing army and excise, have not yet happened: but it does not follow from thence, that they will not happen. The inside of a house may catch fire, and the most valuable apartments be ruined, before the flames[125] burst out. The question in these cases is not, what evil has actually attended particular measures—but what evil, in the nature of things, is likely to attend them. Certain circumstances may for some time delay effects, that were reasonably expected, and that must ensue. There was a long period, after the Romans had prorogued the command to[55]Q. Publilius Philo, before that example destroyed their liberty. All our kings, from the revolution to the present reign have been foreigners. Their ministers generally continued but a short time in authority;[56] and they themselves were mild and virtuous princes.

A bold, ambitious Prince, possessed of great abilities, firmly fixed in the throne by descent, served by ministers like himself, and rendered either venerable or terrible by the glory of his successes, may execute what his[126] predecessors did not dare to attempt. Henry IV. tottered in his seat during his whole reign. Henry V. drew the strength of the kingdom into France, to carry on his wars there, and left the Commons at home, protesting, "that the people were not bound to serve out of the realm."

It is true, that a strong spirit of liberty subsists at present in Great-Britain, but what reliance is to be placed in the temper of a people, when the prince is possessed of an unconstitutional power, our own history can sufficiently inform us. When Charles II. had strengthened himself by the return of the garrison of Tangier, "England (says Rapin) saw on a sudden an amazing revolution; saw herself stripped of all her rights and privileges, excepting such as the King should vouchsafe to grant her; and what is more astonishing, the English themselves delivered up these very rights and privileges to Charles II. which they had so passionately, and, if I may say it, furiously defended against the designs of Charles I." This happened only thirty-six years after this last prince had been beheaded.

Some persons are of opinion, that liberty is not violated, but by such open acts of force; but they seem to be greatly mistaken. I could mention a period within these forty years, when almost as great a change of disposition was produced by the secret measures of a long administration, as by[127] Charles's violence. Liberty, perhaps is never exposed to so much danger, as when the people believe there is the least; for it may be subverted, and yet they not think so.

Public-disgusting acts are seldom practised by the ambitious, at the beginning of their designs. Such conduct silences and discourages the weak, and the wicked, who would otherways have been their advocates or accomplices. It is of great consequence, to allow those, who, upon any account, are inclined to favour them, something specious to say in their defence. The power may be fully established, though it would not be safe for them to do whatever they please. For there are things, which, at some times, even slaves will not bear. Julius Cæsar and Oliver Cromwell did not dare to assume the title of King. The grand Seignior dares not lay a new tax. The King of France dares not be a protestant. Certain popular points may be left untouched, and yet freedom be extinguished. The commonality of Venice imagine themselves free, because they are permitted to do, what they ought not. But I quit a subject, that would lead me too far from my purpose.

By the late act of parliament, taxes are to be levied upon us, for "defraying the charge of the administration of justice, the support of civil government—and the expences of defending his Majesty's dominions in America."

[128]

If any man doubts what ought to be the conduct of these colonies on this occasion, I would ask them these questions.

Has not the parliament expressly avowed their intention of raising money from us for certain purposes? Is not this scheme popular in Great-Britain? Will the taxes, imposed by the late act, answer those purposes? If it will, must it not take an immense sum from us? If it will not, is it to be expected, that the parliament will not fully execute their intention, when it is pleasing at home, and not opposed here? Must not this be done by imposing new taxes? Will not every addition, thus made to our taxes, be an addition to the power of the British legislature, by increasing the number of officers employed in the collection? Will not every additional tax therefore render it more difficult to abrogate any of them? When a branch of revenue is once established, does it not appear to many people invidious and undutiful, to attempt to abolish it? If taxes, sufficient to accomplish the intention of the Parliament, are imposed by the Parliament, what taxes will remain to be imposed by our assemblies? If no material taxes remain to be imposed by them, what must become of them, and the people they represent? [57] "If any person considers, these things,[129] and yet not thinks our liberties are in danger, I wonder at that person's security."

One other argument is to be added, which, by itself, I hope, will be sufficient to convince the most incredulous man on this continent, that the late act of Parliament is only designed to be a precedent, whereon the future vassalage of these colonies may be established.

Every duty thereby laid on articles of British manufacture, is laid on some commodity upon the exportation of which from Great-Britain, a drawback is payable. Those drawbacks in most of the articles, are exactly double to the duties given by the late act. The Parliament therefore might in half a dozen lines have raised much more money only by stopping the drawbacks in the hands of the officers at home, on exportation to these colonies, than by this solemn imposition of taxes upon us, to be collected here. Probably, the artful contrivers of this act formed it in this manner, in order to reserve to themselves, in case of any objections being made to it, this specious pretence—"That the drawbacks are gifts to the colonies; and that the act only lessens those gifts." But the truth is, that the drawbacks are intended for the encouragement and promotion of British manufactures and commerce, and are allowed on exportation to any foreign parts, as well as on exportation to these provinces. Besides, care[130] has been taken to slide into the act[58] some articles on which there are no drawbacks. However, the whole duties laid by the late act on all the articles therein specified, are so small, that they will not amount to as much as the drawbacks which are allowed on part of them only. If, therefore, the sum to be obtained by the late act had been the sole object in forming it, there would not have been any occasion for the "Commons of Great-Britain to give and grant to his Majesty, rates and duties for raising a revenue in his Majesty's dominions in America, for making a more certain and adequate provision for defraying the charge of the administration of justice, the support of civil government, and the expences of defending the said dominions"——Nor would there have been any occasion for an[59]expensive board of commissioners,[131] and all the other new charges to which we are made liable.

Upon the whole, for my part, I regard the late act as an experiment made of our disposition. It is a bird sent over the waters, to discover, whether the waves, that lately agitated this part of the world with such violence, are yet subsided. If this adventurer gets footing here, we shall quickly be convinced, that it is not a phenix; for we shall soon see it followed by others of the same kind. We shall find it rather to be of the[60]breed described by the poet—

"*Infelix vates.*"

A direful foreteller of future calamities.

A FARMER.

[132]

[133]

LETTER XII.

Beloved Countrymen,

Some states have lost their liberty by particular accidents; but this calamity is generally owing to the decay of virtue. A people is travelling fast to destruction, when individuals consider their interests as distinct from those of the public. Such notions are fatal to their country, and to themselves. Yet how many are there so weak and sordid as to think they perform all the offices of life, if they earnestly endeavour to increase their own wealth, power, and credit, without the least regard for the society, under the protection of which they live; who, if they can make an immediate profit to themselves, by lending their assistance to those, whose projects plainly tend to the injury of their country, rejoice in their dexterity, and believe themselves intitled to the character of able politicians. Miserable men! of whom it is hard to say, whether they ought to be most the objects of pity or contempt, but whose opinions are certainly as detestable as their practices are destructive.

Though I always reflect with a high pleasure on the integrity and understanding of[134] my countrymen, which, joined with a pure and humble devotion to the great and gracious author of every blessing they enjoy, will, I hope, ensure to them, and their posterity, all temporal and eternal happiness; yet when I consider, that in every age and country there have been bad men, my heart, at this threatening period, is so full of apprehension, as not to permit me to believe, but that there may be some on this continent, against whom you ought to be upon your guard. Men, who either[61]hold or expect[135] to hold certain advantages by setting examples of servility to their countrymen—Men who trained to the employment, or self-taught by a natural versatility of genius, serve as decoys for drawing the innocent and unwary into snares. It is not to be[136] doubted but that such men will diligently bestir themselves, on this and every like occasion, to spread the infection of their meanness as far as they can. On the plans they have adopted, this is their course. This is the method to recommend themselves to their patrons.

They act consistently, in a bad cause.

They run well in a mean race.

From them we shall learn, how pleasant and profitable a thing it is, to be, for our submissive behaviour, well spoken of in St. James's, or St. Stephen's; at Guildhall, or the Royal Exchange. Specious fallacies will be drest up with all the arts of delusion, to persuade one colony to distinguish herself from another, by unbecoming condescensions, which will serve the ambitious purpose of great men at home, and therefore will be thought by them, to entitle their assistants in obtaining them, to considerable rewards.

Our fears will be excited; our hopes will be awakened. It will be insinuated to us with a plausible affectation of wisdom and concern, how prudent it is to please the powerful—how dangerous to provoke them—and then comes in the perpetual incantation, that freezes up every generous purpose of the soul, in cold—inactive—expectation "that if there is any request to be made, compliance will obtain a favourable attention."

[137]

Our vigilance and our union are success and safety. Our negligence and our division are distress and death. They are worse—they are shame and slavery.

Let us equally shun the benumbing stillness of overweening sloth, and the feverish activity of that ill-informed zeal, which buries itself in maintaining little, mean, and narrow opinions. Let us, with a truly wise generosity and charity, banish and discourage all illiberal distinctions, which may arise from differences in situation, forms of government, or modes of religion. Let us consider ourselves as men—Freemen—Christian men—separated from the rest of the world, and firmly bound together by the same rights, interests, and dangers. Let these keep our attention inflexibly fixed on the great objects, which we must continually regard, in order to preserve those rights, to promote those interests, and to avert those dangers.

Let these truths be indelibly impressed on our minds—that we cannot be happy without being free—that we cannot be free without being secure in our property—that we cannot be secure in our property, if, without our consent, others may, as by right, take it away—that taxes imposed on us by parliament, do thus take it away—that duties laid for the sole purposes of raising money, are taxes—that attempts to lay such[138] duties should be instantly and firmly opposed—that this opposition can never be effectual, unless it is the united effort of these provinces—that, therefore, benevolence of temper toward each other, and unanimity of counsels are essential to the welfare of the whole—and lastly, that, for this reason, every man amongst us, who, in any manner, would encourage either dissention, diffidence, or indifference between these colonies, is an enemy to himself and to his country.

The belief of these truths, I verily think, my countrymen, is indispensably necessary to your happiness. I beseech you, therefore,[62] "Teach them diligently unto your children, and talk of them when you sit in your houses, and when you walk by the way, and when you lie down, and when you rise up."

What have these colonies to ask, while they continue free? Or what have they to dread, but insidious attempts to subvert their freedom? Their prosperity does not depend on ministerial favours doled out to particular provinces. They form one political body, of which each colony is a member. Their happiness is founded on their constitution; and is to be promoted by preserving that constitution in unabated vigour throughout every part. A spot, a speck of decay, however small the limb on[139] which it appears, and however remote it may seem from the vitals, should be alarming. We have all the rights requisite for our prosperity. The legal authority of Great-Britain may indeed lay hard restrictions upon us; but, like the spear of Telephus, it will cure as well as wound. Her unkindness will instruct and compel us, after some time, to discover, in our industry and frugality, surprising remedies— if our rights continue inviolated. For as long as the products of our labours and the rewards of our care, can properly be called our own, so long will it be worth our while to be industrious and frugal. But if when we plow—sow—reap—gather—and thresh, we find, that we plow—sow—reap—gather—and thresh for others, whose pleasure is to be the sole limitation, how much they shall take, and how much they shall leave, why should we repeat the unprofitable toil? Horses and oxen are content with that portion of the fruits of their work, which their owners assign to them, in order to keep them strong enough to raise successive crops; but even these beasts will not submit to draw for their masters, until they are subdued with whips and goads. Let us take care of our rights, and we therein take care of our property. "Slavery is ever preceded by sleep."[63] Individuals may be dependant on ministers, if[140] they please. States should scorn it——And, if you are not wanting to yourselves, you will have a proper regard paid you by those, to whom if you are not respectable, you will infallibly be contemptible. But if we have already forgot the reasons that urged us, with unexampled unanimity, to exert ourselves two years ago; if our zeal for the public good is worn out before the homespun cloaths which it caused us to have made—if our resolutions are so faint, as by our present conduct to condemn our own late successful example——if we are not affected by any reverence for the memory of our ancestors, who transmitted to us that freedom in which they had been blest——if we are not animated by any regard for posterity, to whom, by the most sacred obligations, we are bound to deliver down the invaluable inheritance—Then, indeed, any minister—or any tool of a minister—or any creature of a tool of a minister—or any lower[64]instrument of administration, if lower[141] there may be, is a personage, whom it may be dangerous to offend.

I shall be extremely sorry if any man mistakes my meaning in any thing I have said. Officers employed by the crown, are, while according to the laws they conduct themselves,[142] entitled to legal obedience and sincere respect. These it is a duty to render them, and these no good or prudent person will withhold. But when these officers, thro' rashness or design, endeavour to enlarge their authority beyond its due limits, and expect improper concessions to be made to them, from regard for the employments they bear, their attempts should be considered as equal injuries to the crown and people, and should be courageously and constantly opposed. To suffer our ideas to be confounded by names, on such occasions, would certainly be an inexcusable weakness, and probably, an irremediable error.

We have reason to believe, that several of his Majesty's present ministers are good men, and friends to our country; and it seems not unlikely, that by a particular concurrence of events, we have been treated a little more severely than they wished we[143]should be. They might not think it prudent to stem a torrent. But what is the difference to us, whether arbitrary acts take their rise from ministers, or are permitted by them? Ought any point to be allowed to a good[65] minister, that should be denied to a bad one? The mortality of ministers is a very frail mortality. A * * * may succeed a Shelburne—a * * * may succeed a Conway.

We find a new kind of minister lately spoken of at home——"The minister of the house of Commons." The term seems to have particular propriety when referred to these colonies, with a different meaning annexed to it, from that in which it is taken there. By the word "minister" we may understand not only a servant of the crown, but a man of influence among the Commons, who regard themselves as having a share of the sovereignty over us.

The minister of the house may, in a point respecting the colonies, be so strong, that the minister of the crown in the house, if he is a distinct person, may not chuse, even where his sentiments are favourable to us, to come to a pitched battle upon our account. For tho' I have the highest opinion of the deference of the house for the King's minister; yet he[144] may be so good natured as not to put it to the test, except it be for the mere and immediate profit of his master or himself.

But whatever kind of minister he is, that attempts to innovate a single iota in the privileges of these colonies, him I hope you will undauntedly oppose, and that you will never suffer yourselves to be either cheated or frightened into any unworthy obsequiousness. On such emergencies you may surely without presumption believe that ALMIGHTY GOD himself will look down upon your righteous contest with gracious approbation. You will be a "Band of brother's" cemented by the dearest ties—and strengthened with inconceivable supplies of force and constancy, by that sympathetic ardour which animates good men, confederated in a good cause. Your honour and welfare will be, as they now are, most intimately concerned; and besides——you are assigned by Divine Providence, in the appointed order of things, the protectors of unborn ages, whose fate depends upon your virtue. Whether they shall arise the noble and indisputable heirs of the richest patrimonies, or the dastardly and hereditary drudges of imperious task-masters, you must determine.

To discharge this double duty to yourselves and to your posterity; you have nothing to do, but to call forth into use the good sense and spirit, of which you are possessed. You have nothing to do, but to conduct your[145] affairs peaceably——prudently——firmly——jointly. By these means you will support the character of freemen, without losing that of faithful subjects—a good character in any government—one of the best under a British government. You will prove that Americans have that true magnanimity of soul, that can resent injuries without falling into rage; and that tho' your devotion to Great-Britain is the most affectionate, yet you can make proper distinctions, and know what you owe to yourselves as well as to her——you will, at the same time that you advance your interests, advance your reputation—you will convince the world of the justice of your demands, and the purity of your intentions—while all mankind must with unceasing applauses confess, that you indeed deserve liberty, who so well understand it, so passionately love it, so temperately enjoy it, and so wisely, bravely, and virtuously, assert, maintain, and defend it.

"*Certe ego libertatem quæ mihi a parente meo tradita est, experiar, verum id frustra, an ob rem faciam, in vestra manu situm est, quirites.*"

"For my part, I am resolved strenuously to contend for the liberty delivered down to me from my ancestors; but whether I shall do this effectually or not, depends on you, my countrymen."

[146]

How little soever one is able to write, yet, when the liberties of one's country are threatened, it is still more difficult to be silent.

A FARMER.

Is there not the greatest reason to hope, if the universal sense of the colonies is immediately exprest by resolves of the assemblies, in support of their rights; by instructions to their agents on the subject; and by petitions to the crown and parliament for redress; that those measures will have the same success now that they had in the time of the Stamp-act.

To the ingenious Author of certain patriotic Letters, subscribed A FARMER.

MUCH RESPECTED SIR,

When the rights and liberties of the numerous and loyal inhabitants of this extensive continent are in imminent danger,—when the inveterate enemies of these colonies are not more assiduous to forge fetters for them, than diligent to delude the people, and zealous to persuade them to an indolent acquiescence: At this alarming period, when to reluct is deemed a revolt, and to oppose such measures as are injudicious and destructive, is construed as a formal attempt to subvert order and government; when to reason is to rebel; and a ready submission to the rod of power, is sollicited by the tenders of place and patronage, or urged by the menace of danger and disgrace: 'Tis to YOU, worthy SIR, that AMERICA is obliged, for a most seasonable, sensible, loyal, and vigorous vindication of her invaded rights and liberties: 'Tis to YOU, the distinguished honour is due; that when many of the friends of liberty were ready to fear its utter subversion: Armed with truth, supported by the immutable laws of nature, the common inheritance of man, and leaning on the pillars of the BRITISH constitution; you seasonably brought your aid, opposed impending ruin, awakened the most indolent and inactive, to a sense of danger, re-animated the hopes of those, who had before exerted themselves in the cause of freedom, and instructed AMERICA in the best means to obtain redress.

Nor is this western world alone indebted to your wisdom, fortitude, and patriotism:GREAT-BRITAIN also may be confirmed by you, that to be truly great and successful, she must be just: That to oppress AMERICA, is to violate her own honours, defeat her brightest prospects, and contract her spreading empire.

To such eminent worth and virtue, the inhabitants of the town of BOSTON, the capital of the province of the MASSACHUSETTS-BAY, in full town meeting assembled, express their earliest gratitude. Actuated themselves by the same generous principles, which appear with so much lustre in your useful labours, they will not fail warmly to recommend, and industriously to promote that union among the several colonies, which is so indispensably necessary for the security of the whole.

Tho' such superior merit must assuredly, in the closest recess, enjoy the divine satisfaction of having served, and possibly saved this people; tho' veiled from our view, you modestly shun the deserved applause of millions; permit us to intrude upon your retirement, and salute The FARMER, as the FRIEND OF AMERICANS, and the common benefactor of mankind.

Boston, March 22, 1768.

The above letter was read, and unanimously accepted by the town, and ordered to be published in the several news-papers.

Attest. WILLIAM COOPER, Town-Clerk.

FOOTNOTES:

[1]"The Life and Times of John Dickinson," by Charles J. Stillé.

[2]The "Address from the Town of Providence," printed from the original manuscript, is to be found in the Notes, page li.

[3]Two weeks later a letter of thanks voted by the town of Boston was added to this edition.

[4]The Song has been given already in our Chronicle.

[5]Reproduced through the courtesy of the Library Company of Philadelphia. I wish also to express my obligation to my friends Messrs. Wilberforce Eames of the Lenox Library and Robert H. Kelby of the New York Historical Society for repeated access to the volumes of Colonial Newspapers, etc., in the collections under their charge.

[6]The Name at length.

[7]Of Pennsylvania. See his dispute with Mr. Galloway, Review, vol. xxxii. p. 67.

[8]POPE.

[9]For the satisfaction of the reader, recitals from former acts of parliament relating to these colonies are added. By comparing these with the modern acts, he will perceive their great difference in expression and intention.

The 12th Cha. II Chap. 18, which forms the foundation of the laws relating to our trade, by enacting that certain productions of the colonies shall be carried to England only, and that no goods shall be imported from the plantations but in ships belonging to England, Ireland, Wales, Berwick, or the Plantations, &c. begins thus: "For the increase of shipping, and encouragement of the navigation of this nation, wherein, under the good providence and protection of God, the wealth, safety, and strength of this kingdom is so much concerned," &c.

The 15th Cha. II. Chap. 7. enforcing the same regulation, assigns these reasons for it. "In regard to his Majesty's plantations, beyond the seas, are inhabited and peopled by his subjects of this his kingdom of England; for the maintaining a greater correspondence and kindness between them, and keeping them in a firmer dependence upon it, and rendering them yet more beneficial and advantageous unto it, in the further employment and increase of English shipping and seamen, vent of English woolen, and other manufactures and commodities, rendering the navigation to and from the same more safe and cheap, and making this kingdom a staple, not only of the commodities of those plantations, but also of the commodities of other countries and places for the supplying of them; and it being the usage of other nations to keep their plantations trade to themselves," &c.

The 25th Cha. II. Chap. 7, made expressly "for the better securing the plantation trade," which imposes duties on certain commodities exported from one colony to another, mentions this last for imposing them: "Whereas by one act passed in the 12th year of your Majesty's reign, intitled, an act for encouragement of shipping and navigation, and by several other laws, passed since that time, it is permitted to ship, &c. sugars, tobacco, &c. of the growth, &c. of any of your Majesty's plantations in America &c. from the places of their growth, &c. to any other of your Majesty's plantations in those parts, &c. and that without paying of custom for the same, either at the lading or unlading the said commodities, by means whereof the trade and navigation in those commodities from one plantation to another is greatly encreased, and the inhabitants of divers of those colonies, not contenting themselves with being supplied with those commodities for their own use, free from all customs (while the subjects of this your kingdom of England have paid great customs and impositions for what of them hath been spent here) but, contrary to the express letter of the aforesaid laws, have brought into diverse parts of Europe great quantities thereof, and do also vend great quantities thereof to the shipping of other nations, who bring them into divers parts of Europe, to the great hurt and diminution of your Majesty's customs, and of the trade and navigation of this your kingdom; for the prevention thereof, &c."

The 7th and 8th Will. III. Chap. 21, intitled, "An act for preventing frauds, and regulating abuses in the plantation trade," recites that, "notwithstanding diverse acts, &c. great abuses are daily committed, to the prejudice of the English navigation, and the loss of a great part of the plantation trade to this kingdom, by the artifice and cunning of ill disposed persons: for remedy whereof, &c. And whereas in some of his Majesty's American plantations, a doubt or misconstruction has arisen upon the before mentioned acts, made in the 25th year of the reign of Charles II. whereby certain duties are laid upon the commodities therein enumerated (which by law may be transported from one plantation to another, for the supplying of each others wants) as if the same were, by the payment of those duties in one plantation, discharged from giving the securities intended by the aforesaid acts, made in the 12th, 22d and 23d years of the reign of King Charles II. and consequently be at liberty to go to any foreign market in Europe," &c.

The 6th Anne, Chap. 37, reciting the advancement of trade, &c. and encouragement of ships of war, &c. grants to the captors the property of all prizes carried into America, subject to such customs and duties, &c. as if the same had been first imported into any part of Great-Britain, and from thence exported, &c.

This was a gift to persons acting under commissions from the crown, and therefore it was reasonable that the terms prescribed should be complied with————more especially as the payment of such duties was intended to give a preference to the productions of the British colonies, over those of other colonies. However, being found inconvenient to the colonies, about four years afterwards, this act was, for that reason, so far repealed, by another act "all prize goods, imported into any part of Great-Britain, from any of the plantations, were liable to such duties only in Great-Britain, as in case they had been of the growth and produce of the plantations," &c.

The 6th Geo. II. Chap. 13, which imposes duties on foreign rum, sugar and molasses, imported into the colonies, shews the reason thus.—"Whereas the welfare and prosperity of your Majesty's sugar colonies in America, are of the greatest consequence and importance to the trade, navigation and strength of this kingdom; and whereas the planters of the said sugar colonies, have of late years fallen under such great discouragements that they are unable to improve or carry on the sugar trade, upon an equal footing with the foreign sugar colonies, without some advantage and relief be given to them from Great-Britain: For remedy whereof, and for the good and welfare of your Majesty's subjects," &c.

The 29th Geo. II. Chap. 26. and the 1st Geo. III. Chap. 9, which contains 6th Geo. II. Chap. 13, declare, that the said act hath, by experience, been found useful and beneficial, &c. There are all the most considerable statutes relating to the commerce of the colonies; and it is thought to be utterly unnecessary to add any observations to these extracts, to prove that they were all intended solely as regulations of trade.

[10]It is worthy observation how quickly subsidies, granted in forms usual and accustomable (tho' heavy) are borne; such a power hath use and custom. On the other side, what discontentment and disturbances subsidies formed on new moulds do raise (such an inbred hatred novelty doth hatch) is evident by examples of former times. Lord Coke's 2d institute, p. 33.

[11]Some people, whose minds seem incapable of uniting two ideas, think that Great-Britain has the same right to impose duties on the exports to these colonies, as on those to Spain and Portugal, &c. Such persons attend so much to the idea of exportation, that they entirely drop that of the connection between the mother country and her colonies. If Great-Britain had always claimed, and exercised an authority to compel Spain and Portugal to import manufactures from her only, the cases would be parallel: But as she never pretended to such a right, they are at liberty to get them where they please; and if they chuse to take them from her, rather than from other nations, they voluntary consent to pay the duties imposed on them.

[12]The peasants of France wear wooden shoes; and the vassals of Poland are remarkable for matted hair, which never can be combed.

[13]Gal. v. 1.

[14]Cleon was a popular firebrand of Athens and Clodius of Rome; each of them plunged his country into the deepest calamities.

[15]It is very worthy of remark, how watchful our wise ancestors were, least these services should be extended beyond the limits of the law. No man was bound to go out of the realm to serve, and therefore even in the conquering reign of Henry V. when the martial spirit of the nation was inflamed by success to a great degree, they still carefully guarded against the establishment of illegal services. Lord Chief Justice Coke's words are these, "When this point concerning maintainance of wars out of England came in question, the Commons did make their continual claim of their antient freedom and birth-right, as in the first of Henry V. and 7th of Henry V. &c. the Commons made protest that they were not bound to the maintainance of war in Scotland, Ireland, Calais, France, Normandy, or other foreign parts, and caused their protests to be entered into the parliament roll, where they yet remain; which, in effect, agreeth with that, which upon the like occasion was made in the parliament of 25. E. 1." 2d Inst. p. 528.

[16]4. Inst. p. 28.

[17]*Rege Angliæ nihiltale, nisi convocatis primis ordinibus et assentiente populo, suscipiunt. Phil. Comines.*

These gifts entirely depending on the pleasure of the donors, were proportioned to the abilities of the several ranks of people, who gave, and were regulated by their opinion of the public necessities. Thus Edward I. had in his 11th year a thirteenth from the laity, a twentieth from the clergy; in his 22d year, a tenth from the laity, a sixth from London, and other corporate towns, half of their benefices from the clergy; in his 23d year, an eleventh from the barons and others, a tenth from the clergy, and a seventh from the burgesses, &c.

Hume's History of England.

The same difference in the grants of the several ranks, is observable in other reigns. In the famous statute *de tallagio non concedendo*, the King enumerates the several classes, without whose consent he and his heirs should never set or levy any tax. "*Nullum tallagium vel auxilium, per nos, vel hæredes nostros, in regno nostro ponatur seu levetur, sine voluntare et assensu archiepiscoporum, episcoporum, comitum, baronum, militum, burgensium, et aliorum liberorum de regno nostro.*" 34 E. I.

Lord Chief Justice Coke in his comment on these words, says, "for the quieting of the Commons, and for a perpetual and constant law for ever after, both in this and other like cases, this act was made." "These words are plain without scruple; absolute without any saving."

2 Coke's Inst. p. 522, 523.

Little did the venerable judge imagine, that "other like cases" would happen, in which the spirit of this law would be despised by Englishmen, the posterity of those who made it.

[18]4. Inst. p. 28.

[19]The goddess of empire, in the heathen mythology. According to an ancient fable, Ixion pursued her, but she escaped by a cloud which she threw in his way.

[20]In this sense Montesquieu uses the word "tax", in his 13th book of Spirit of Laws.

[21]It seems to be evident, that Mr. Pitt, in his defence of America, during the debate concerning the repeal of the Stamp-act, by "*internal taxes*" meant any duties "*for the purpose of raising a revenue*," and by "*external taxes*," meant "*duties imposed for the regulation of trade*." His expressions are these.—"If the gentleman does not understand the difference between internal and external taxes, I cannot help it; but there is a plain distinction between taxes levied for the purposes of raising a revenue, and duties imposed for the regulation of trade, for the accommodation of the subject; altho' in the consequences, some revenue might incidentally arise from the latter."

These words were in Mr. Pitt's reply to Mr. Grenville, who said he could not understand the difference between external and internal taxes. But Mr. Pitt in his first speech, had made no such distinction; and his meaning, when he mentions the distinction, appears to be—that by "*external taxes*," he intended impositions, for the purpose of regulating the intercourse of the colonies with others; and by "*internal taxes*," he intended impositions, for the purpose of taking money from them.

In every other part of his speeches on that occasion, his words confirm this construction of his expressions. The following extracts will shew how positive and general were his assertions of our right.

"IT IS MY OPINION THAT THIS KINGDOM HAS NO RIGHT TO LAY A TAX UPON THE COLONIES." "THE AMERICANS ARE THE SONS NOT THE BASTARDS OF ENGLAND. TAXATION IS NO PART OF THE GOVERNING OR LEGISLATIVE POWER." "The taxes are a voluntary gift and grant of the Commons alone. In legislation the three estates of the realm are alike concerned, but the concurrence of the peers and the crown to a tax, is only necessary to close with the form of a law. The gift and grant is of the Commons alone." "The distinction between legislation and taxation is essentially necessary to liberty." "*The Commons of America represented in their several assemblies have ever been in possession of the exercise of this, their constitutional right, of giving and granting their own money. They would have been slaves, if they had not enjoyed it.*" "The idea of a virtual representation of America in this house, is the most contemptible idea that ever entered into the head of man. It does not deserve a serious refutation."

He afterwards shews the unreasonableness of Great-Britain taxing America, thus— "When I had the honour of serving his Majesty, I availed myself of the means of information, which I derived from my office: I speak therefore from knowledge. My materials were good, I was at pains to collect, to digest, to consider them: *and I will be bold to affirm that the profit to Great-Britain from the trade of the colonies, thro' all its branches, is two millions a year. This is the fund that carried you triumphantly thro' the last war.* The estates that were rented at two thousand pounds a year, threescore years ago, are at three thousand pounds at present. Those estates sold then from fifteen to eighteen years purchase; the same may now be sold for thirty. YOU OWE THIS TO AMERICA. THIS IS THE PRICE THAT AMERICA PAYS YOU FOR HER PROTECTION,"—"I dare not say how much higher these profits may be augmented."—"Upon the whole, I will beg leave to tell the house what is really my opinion: it is, THAT THE STAMP-ACT BE REPEALED ABSOLUTELY, TOTALLY, AND IMMEDIATELY. That the reason for the repeal be assigned, because it was founded on an erroneous principle."

[22]"And that pig and bar iron made in his Majesty's colonies in America may be further manufactured in this kingdom, be it further enacted by the authority aforesaid, that

from and after the twenty-fourth day of June, 1750, no mill or other engine for slitting or rolling of iron, or any plaiting forge to work with a tilt hammer, or any furnace for making steel, shall be erected, or after such erection continued, in any of his Majesty's colonies in America."

3 Geo. II. chap. 29. sect. 9.

[23]Though these particulars are mentioned as being so absolutely necessary, yet perhaps they are not more so than glass, in our severe winters, to keep out the cold, from our houses; or than paper, without which such inexpressible confusion must ensue.

[24]The power of taxing themselves, was the privileges of which the English were, with reason, particularly jealous.

Hume's hist. of England.

[25]Mic. iv. 4.

[26]It has been said in the house of commons, when complaints have been made of the decay of trade to any part of Europe, "That such things were not worth regard, as Great-Britain was possest of colonies that could consume more of her manufactures than she was able to supply them with."

"As the case now stands, we shall shew that the plantations are a spring of wealth to this nation, that they work for us, that their treasure centers all here, and that the laws have tied them fast enough to us; so that it must be through our own fault and mismanagement, if they become independent of England."

Davenant on the plantat. trade.

"It is better that the islands should be supplied from the Northern Colonies than from England, for this reason; the provisions we might send to Barbados, Jamaica, &c. would be unimproved product of the earth, as grain of all kinds, or such product where there is little got by the improvement, as malt, salt, beef and pork; indeed the exportation of salt fish thither would be more advantageous, but the goods which we send to the northern colonies are such, whose improvement may be justly said, one with another to be near four fifths of the value of the whole commodity, as apparel, household furniture, and many other things."

Idem.

"New-England is the most prejudicial plantation to the kingdom of England; and yet, to do right to that most industrious English colony, I must confess, that though we lose by their unlimited trade with other foreign plantations, yet we are very great gainers by their direct trade to and from Old England. Our yearly exportations of English manufactures, malt and other goods, from hence thither, amounting, in my opinion, to ten times the value of what is imported from thence; which calculation I do not make at random, but upon mature consideration, and peradventure, upon as much experience in this very trade, as any other person will pretend to; and therefore, whenever reformation of our correspondency in trade with that people shall be thought on, it will, in my poor judgment, require great tenderness, and very serious circumspection."

Sir Josiah Child's discourse on trade.

"Our plantations spend mostly our English manufactures, and those of all sorts almost imaginable, in egregious quantities, and employ near two thirds of all our English shipping; so that we have more people in England, by reason of our plantations in America."

Idem.

Sir Josiah Child says, in another part of his work, "that not more than fifty families are maintained in England by the refining of sugar." From whence, and from what Davenant says, it is plain, that the advantages here said to be derived from the plantations by England, must be meant chiefly of the continental colonies.

"I shall sum up my whole remarks on our American colonies, with this observation, that as they are a certain annual revenue of several millions sterling to their mother country, they ought carefully to be protected, duly encouraged, and every opportunity that presents, improved for their increasment and advantage, as every one they can possibly reap, must at least return to us with interest."

Beawes's Lex merc. red.

"We may safely advance, that our trade and navigation are greatly increased by our colonies, and that they really are a source of treasure and naval power to this kingdom, since they work for us, and their treasure centers here. Before their settlement, our manufactures were few, and those but indifferent; the number of English merchants very small, and the whole shipping of the nation much inferior to what now belongs to the northern colonies only. These are certain facts. But since their establishment, our condition has altered for the better, almost to a degree beyond credibility. Our manufactures are prodigiously encreased, chiefly by the demand for them in the plantations, where they at least take off one half, and supply us with many valuable commodities for exportation, which is as great an emolument to the mother kingdom, as to the plantations themselves."

Postlethwait's universal dict. of trade and commerce.

"Most of the nations of Europe have interfered with us more or less, in divers of our staple manufactures, within half a century, not only in our woollen, but in our lead and tin manufactures, as well as our fisheries."

Idem.

"The inhabitants of our colonies, by carrying on a trade with their foreign neighbours, do not only occasion a greater quantity of the goods and merchandizes of Europe being sent from hence to them, and a greater quantity of the product of America to be sent from them thither, which would otherways be carried from, and brought to Europe by foreigners, but an increase of the seamen and navigation in those parts, which is of great strength and security, as well as of great advantage to our plantations in general. And though some of our colonies are not only for preventing the importations of all goods of the same species they produce, but suffer particular planters to keep great runs of land in their possession uncultivated with design to prevent new settlements, whereby they imagine the prices of their commodities may be affected; yet if it be considered, that the markets of Great-Britain depend on the markets of all Europe in general, and that the European markets in general depend on the proportion between the annual consumption and the whole quantity of each species annually produced by all nations; it must follow, that whether we or foreigners, are the producers, carriers, importers and exporters of American produce, yet their respective prices in each colony (the difference of freight, customs and importations considered) will always bear proportion to the general consumption of the whole quantity of each sort, produced in all colonies, and in all parts, allowing only for the usual contingencies, that trade and commerce, agriculture and manufactures are liable to in all countries."

Idem.

"It is certain, that from the very time Sir Walter Raleigh, the father of our English colonies, and his associates, first projected these establishments, there have been persons who have found an interest, in misrepresenting, or lessening the value of them.—The attempts were called chimerical and dangerous. Afterwards many malignant suggestions were made, about sacrificing so many Englishmen to the obstinate desire of settling colonies in countries which then produced very little advantage. But as these difficulties were gradually surmounted, those complaints vanished. No sooner were these lamentations over, but others arose in their stead; when it could be no longer said, that the colonies were useless, it was alledged that they were not useful enough to their mother country; that while we were loaded with taxes, they were absolutely free; that the planters lived like princes, when the inhabitants of England laboured hard for a tolerable subsistence."

Idem.

"Before the settlement of these colonies," says Postlethwayt, "our manufactures were few, and those but indifferent. In those days we had not only our naval stores, but our ships from our neighbours. Germany furnished us with all things made of metal, even to nails. Wine, paper, linens, and a thousand other things came from France. Portugal supplied us with sugar; all the products of America were poured into us from Spain; and the Venetians and Genoese retailed to us the commodities of the East-Indies, at their own price."

"If it be asked, whether foreigners for what goods they take of us, do not pay on that consumption a great portion of our taxes? It is admitted they do."

Postlethwayt's Great-Britain's true system.

"If we are afraid that one day or other the colonies will revolt, and set up for themselves, as some seem to apprehend, let us not drive them to a necessity to feel themselves independant of us; as they will do, the moment they perceive that they can be supplied with all things from within themselves, and do not need our assistance. If we would keep them still dependant upon their mother country, and in some respects subservient to their views and welfare, let us make it their interest always to be so."

Tucker on trade.

"Our colonies, while they have English blood in their veins, and have relations in England, and while they can get by trading with us, the stronger and greater they grow, the more this crown and kingdom will get by them; and nothing but such an arbitrary power as shall make them desperate can bring them to rebel."

Davenant on the plantation trade.

"The northern colonies are not upon the same footing as those of the south; and having a worse soil to improve, they must find the recompence some other way, which only can be in property and dominion. Upon which score, any innovations in the form of government there, should be cautiously examined, for fear of entering upon measures, by which the industry of the inhabitants may be quite discouraged. 'Tis always unfortunate for a people, either by consent or upon compulsion, to depart from their primitive institutions, and those fundamental, by which they were first united together."

Idem.

All wise states will well consider how to preserve the advantages arising from colonies, and avoid the evils. And I conceive that there can be but two ways in nature to hinder them from throwing off their dependence; one to keep it out of their power, and the other, out of their will. The first must be by force; and the latter by using them well, and keeping them employed in such productions, and making such manufactures, as will support themselves and families comfortably, and procure them wealth too, and at least not prejudice their mother country.

Force can never be used effectually to answer the end, without destroying the colonies themselves. Liberty and encouragement are necessary to carry people thither, and to keep them together when they are there; and violence will hinder both. Any body of troops considerable enough to awe them, and keep them in subjection, under the direction too of a needy governor, often sent thither to make his fortune, and at such a distance from any application for redress, will soon put an end to all planting, and leave the country to the soldiers alone, and if it did not, would eat up all the profit of the colony. For this reason, arbitrary countries have not been equally successful in planting colonies with free ones; and what they have done in that kind, has either been by force at a vast expence, or by departing from the nature of their government, and giving such privileges to planters as were denied to their other subjects. And I dare say, that a few prudent laws, and a little prudent conduct, would soon give us far the greatest share of the riches of all America, perhaps drive many of other nations out of it, or into our colonies for shelter.

There are so many exigencies in all states, so many foreign wars and domestic disturbances, that these colonies can never want opportunities, if they watch for them, to do what they shall find their interest to do; and therefore we ought to take all the precautions in our power, that it shall never be their interest to act against that of their native country; an evil which can no otherways be averted, than by keeping them fully employed in such trades as will increase their own, as well as our wealth; for it is much to be feared, if we do not find employment for them, they may find it for us. The interest of the mother country is always to keep them dependent, and so employed; and it requires all her address to do it; and it is certainly more easily and effectually done by gentle and insensible methods, than by power alone.

Cato's letters.

[27]'If any one should observe, that no opposition has been made to the legality of the 4th Geo. III. ch. 15, which is the first act of parliament that ever imposed duties on the importations in America, for the express purpose of raising a revenue there, I answer, first, that tho' that act expressly mentions the raising a revenue in America, yet it seems that it had as much in view, "the improving and securing the trade between the same and Great-

Britain," which words are part of its title, and the preamble says, "Whereas it is expedient that new provisions and regulations should be established for improving the revenue of this kingdom, and for extending and securing the navigation and commerce between Great-Britain and your Majesty's dominions in America, which, by the peace, have been so happily extended and enlarged, &c." 'Secondly, all the duties mentioned in that act, are imposed solely on the productions and manufactures of foreign countries, and not a single duty laid on any production or manufacture of our mother country. Thirdly, the authority of the provincial assemblies is not therein so plainly attacked, as by the last act, which makes provision for defraying the charges of the administration of justice, and the support of civil government, 4thly, That it being doubtful whether the intention of the 4th Geo. III. ch. 15, was not as much to regulate trade as to raise a revenue, the minds of the people here were wholly engrossed by the terror of the Stamp-act, then impending over them, about the intention of which they could be in no doubt.'

'These reasons so far distinguish 4th Geo. III. ch. 15, from the last act, that it is not to be wondered at, that the first should have been submitted to, though the last should excite the most universal and spirited opposition. For this will be found on the strictest examination to be, in the principle on which it is founded, and in the consequences that must attend it, if possible, more destructive than the Stamp-act. It is, to speak plainly, a prodigy in our laws, not having one British feature.'

[28]Tacitus.

[29]2 Cor. iii. 6.

[30]November 5, 1688.

[31]Many remarkable instances might be produced of the extraordinary inattention with which bills of great importance, concerning these colonies, have passed in parliament; which is owing, as it is supposed, to the bills being brought in by the persons who have points to carry, so artfully framed, that it is not easy for the members in general, in the haste of business, to discover their tendency.

The following instances shew the truth of this remark. When Mr. Grenville, in the violence of reformation and innovation, formed the 4th Geo. III. chap. 15th, for regulating the American trade, the word "Ireland" was dropt in the clause relating to our iron and lumber, so that we could send these articles to no other part of Europe, but to Great-Britain. This was so unreasonable a restriction, and so contrary to the sentiments of the legislature, for many years before, that it is surprising it should not have been taken notice of in the house. However the bill passed into a law. But when the matter was explained, this restriction was taken off in a subsequent act.

I cannot postively say, how long after the taking off this restriction, as I have not the acts; but I think in less than eighteen months, another act of parliament passed, in which the word "Ireland," was left out as it had been before. The matter being a second time explained, was a second time regulated.

Now if it be considered, that the omission mentioned struck off, with one word, so very great a part of our trade, it must appear remarkable: and equally so is the method by which rice became an enumerated commodity, and therefore could be carried to Great-Britain only.

"The enumeration was obtained, (says Mr. Gee*) by one Cole, a Captain of a ship, employed by a company then trading to Carolina; for several ships going from England thither and purchasing rice for Portugal, prevented the aforesaid Captain of a loading. Upon his coming home, he possessed one Mr. Lowndes, a member of parliament (who was very frequently employed to prepare bills) with an opinion, that carrying rice directly to Portugal was a prejudice to the trade of England, and privately got a clause into an act to make it an enumerated commodity; by which means he secured a freight to himself. But the consequence proved a vast loss to the nation."

* Gee on trade, p. 32.

[32]Tacitus's An. b. 13. f. 31.

[33]Montesquieu's spirit of laws, b. 13. chap. 8.

[34]Speech Lord Cambden lately published.

[35]This is the opinion of Mr. Pitt, in his speech on the Stamp-act.

"It is my opinion, that this kingdom has no right to lay a tax upon the colonies. The AMERICANS are the SONS, not the BASTARDS of ENGLAND. The distinction between legislation and taxation is essentially necessary to liberty. The Commons of America represented in their several assemblies, have ever been in possession of this their constitutional right of giving and granting their own money. They would have been slaves if they had not enjoyed it. The idea of a virtual representation of America, in this house, is the most contemptible idea that ever entered into the head of man. It does not deserve a serious refutation."

That great and excellent man Lord Cambden, maintains the same opinion in his speech, in the house of peers, on the declaratory bill of the sovereignty of Great-Britain over the colonies. The following extracts so perfectly agree with, and confirm the sentiments avowed in these letters, that it is hoped the inserting them in this note will be excused.

"As the affair is of the utmost importance, and in its consequences may involve the fate of kingdoms, I took the strictest review of my arguments; I re-examined all my authorities; fully determined, if I found myself mistaken, publicly to own my mistake, and give up my opinion, but my searches have more and more convinced me, that the British parliament have no right to tax the Americans. Nor is the doctrine new; it is as old as the constitution; it grew up with it, indeed it is its support. Taxation and representation are inseparably united. God hath joined them; no British parliament can separate them; to endeavour to do it is to stab our vitals.

"My position is this—I repeat it—I will maintain it to my last hour—Taxation and representation are inseparable. This position is founded on the laws of nature; it is more, it is itself an eternal law of nature; for whatever is a man's own, is absolutely his own; and no man hath a right to take it from him without his consent, either expressed by himself or representative; whoever attempts to do it, attempts an injury; whoever does it, commits a robbery; he throws down the distinction between liberty and slavery." "There is not a blade of grass, in the most obscure corner of the kingdom, which is not, which was not, represented since the constitution began: there is not a blade of grass, which when taxed, was not taxed by the consent of the proprietor." "The forefathers of the Americans did not leave their native country, and subject themselves to every danger and distress, to be reduced to the state of slavery. They did not give up their rights; they looked for protection, and not for chains, from their mother-country. By her they expected to be defended in the possession of their property; and not to be deprived of it: For should the present power continue, there is nothing which they can call their own, or, to use the words of Mr. Locke, what property have they in that, which another may, by right, take, when he pleases, to him self."

It is impossible to read this speech and Mr. Pitt's, and not be charmed with the generous zeal for the rights of mankind, that glows in every sentence. These great and good men, animated by the subject they speak upon, seem to rise above all the former glorious exertions of their abilities. A foreigner might be tempted to think they are Americans, asserting with all the ardour of patriotism, and all the anxiety of apprehension, the cause of their native land, and not Britons striving to stop their mistaken countrymen from oppressing others. There reasoning is not only just; it is "vehement," as Mr. Hume says of the eloquence of Demosthenes, "'Tis disdain, anger, boldness, freedom, involved in a continual stream of argument." Hume's Essay on Eloquence.

[36]"So credulous, as well as obstinate, are the people in believing every thing, which flatters their prevailing passion."

Hume's Hist. of England.

[37]Shakespeare.

[38]The writs for searching houses in England are to be granted under the seal of the court of exchequer, according to the statute—and that seal is kept by the chancellor of the exchequer. 4 Inst.

[39]The gentleman must not wonder he was not contradicted, when, as the minister, he asserted the right of parliament to tax America. I know not how it is, but there is a modesty in this house, which does not chuse to contradict a minister. I wish gentlemen

would get the better of that modesty. If they do not, perhaps the collective body may begin to abate of its respect for the representative.

Mr. Pitt's speech.

[40]"Within this act, (*statute de tallagio non concedendo*) are all new offices erected with new fees, or old offices with new fees, for that is a tallage put upon the subject, which cannot be done without common assent by act of parliament."

2 Inst. 533.

[41]An enquiry into the legality of the pensions on the Irish establishment, by Alexander M'Auley, Esq; one of the King's Council, &c.

[42]In Charles II's time, the House of Commons, influenced by some factious demagogues, were resolved to prohibit the importation of Irish cattle into England. Among other arguments in favour of Ireland, it was insisted "That by cutting off almost entirely the trade between the kingdoms, all the natural bands of union were dissolved, and nothing remained to keep the Irish in their duty, but force and violence.

"The King (says Mr. Hume in his History of England) was so convinced of the justice of these reasons, that he used all his interest to oppose the bill, and he openly declared, that he could not give his assent to it with a safe conscience. But the Commons were resolute in their purpose. And the spirit of tyranny, of which nations are as susceptible as individuals, had animated the English extremely to exert their superiority over their dependant state. No affair could be conducted with greater violence that this, by the Commons. They even went so far in the preamble of the bill, as to declare the importation of Irish cattle to be a nuisance. By this expression they gave scope to their passion, and at the same time, barred the King's prerogative, by which he might think intitled to dispense with a law so full of injustice and bad policy. The lords expunged the word, but as the King was sensible that no supply would be given by the Commons, unless they were gratified in all their prejudices, he was obliged both to employ his interest with the Peers to make the bill pass, and to give the Royal assent to it. He could not however forbear expressing his displeasure, at the jealousy entertained against him, and at the intention which the Commons discovered of retrenching his prerogative."

This law brought great distress for sometime upon Ireland, but it occasioned their applying with great industry to manufactures, and has proved, in the issue, beneficial to that kingdom.

Perhaps the same reason occasioned the "barring the King's prerogative" in the late act suspending the legislation of New-York.

This we may be assured of, that we are as dear to his Majesty, as the people of Great-Britain are. We are his subjects as well as they, and as faithful subjects; and his Majesty has given too many, too constant proofs of his piety and virtue, for any man, to think it possible, that such a Prince can make any unjust distinction between such subjects. It makes no difference to his Majesty, whether supplies are raised in Great-Britain, or America: but it makes some difference, to the Commons of that kingdom.

To speak plainly as becomes an honest man on such important occasions, all our misfortunes are owing to a lust of power in men of abilities and influence. This prompts them to seek popularity, by expedients profitable to themselves, though ever so destructive to their country.

Such is the accursed nature of lawless ambition, and yet—what heart but melts at the thought?—Such false detestable patriots in every nation have led their blind confiding country, shouting their applauses, into the jaws of shame and ruin. May the wisdom and goodness of the people of Great-Britain, save them from the usual fate of nations.

[43]The last Irish parliament continued thirty-three years, that is during all the late reign. The present parliament there, has continued from the beginning of this reign; and probably will continue to the end.

[44]I am informed, that within these few years, a petition was presented to the House of Commons in Great-Britain, setting forth, "that herrings were imported into Ireland, from some foreign parts of the north so cheap, as to discourage the British herring fishery, and therefore praying, that some remedy might be applied in that behalf by parliament"—"That, upon this petition, the House resolved to impose a duty of two shillings sterling on every

60

barrel of foreign herrings imported into Ireland, but afterwards dropt the affair, for fear of engaging in a dispute with Ireland about the right of taxing her."

So much higher was the opinion, which the House entertained of the spirit of Ireland, than of that of these colonies.

I find in the last English papers, that the resolution and firmness with which the people of that kingdom have lately asserted their freedom, have been so alarming in Great-Britain, that the Lord Lieutenant in his speech on the 20th of last October, "recommended" to the parliament, "that such provision may be made for securing the judges in the enjoyment of their offices and appointments during their good behaviour, as shall be thought most expedient."

What an important concession is thus obtained by making demands becoming freemen, with a courage and perseverance becoming freemen.

[45]One of the reasons urged by that great and honest statesman, Sir William Temple, to Charles II. in his famous remonstrance to dissuade him from aiming at arbitrary power, was, the "King had few offices to bestow."

Hume's Hist. of England.

"Though the wings of prerogative have been clipt, the influence of the crown is greater than ever it was in any period of our history. For when we consider in how many burroughs the government has the voters at command, when we consider the vast body of persons employed in the collection of the revenue in every part of the kingdom, the inconceivable number of placemen, and candidates for places in the customs, in the excise, in the post-office, in the dock-yards, in the ordnance, in the salt-office, in the stamps, in the navy and victualling offices, and in a variety of other departments; when we consider again the extensive influence of the money corporations, subscription jobbers, and contractors: the endless dependance created by the obligations conferred on the bulk of the gentlemen's families throughout the kingdom, who have relations preferred in our navy and numerous standing army; when, I say, we consider how wide, how binding, a dependance on the crown is created by the above enumerated particulars; and the great, the enormous weight and influence which the crown derives from this extensive dependance upon its favour and power; any lord in waiting, any lord of the bedchamber, any man may be appointed minister."

"A doctrine to this effect is said to have been the advice of L—— H——."

Late News papers.

[46]The people of Maryland and Pennsylvania have been engaged in the warmest disputes, in order to obtain an equal and just taxation of their proprietors estates; but the late act does more for these proprietors than they themselves would venture to demand. It totally exempts them from taxation.

[47]Machiavel's discourses. Book 3, chap. 1.

[48]The author is sensible that this is putting the gentlest construction on Charles' conduct; and that is one reason why he chuses it. Allowance ought to be made for the errors of those men, who are acknowledged to have been possessed of many virtues. The education of that unhappy Prince, and his confidence in men not so good and wise as himself, had probably filled him with mistaken notions of his own authority, and of the consequences that would attend concessions of any kind to a people, who were represented to him as aiming at too much power.

[49]"Opinion is of two kinds, viz. opinion of interest, and opinion of right. By opinion of interest, I chiefly understand, the sense of public advantage which is reaped from government; together with the persuasion, that the particular government which is established, is equally advantageous with any other, that could be easily settled."

"Right is of two kinds, right to power, and right to property. What prevalence opinion of the first kind has over mankind may easily be understood, by observing the attachment which all nations have to their ancient government, and even to those names which have had the sanction of antiquity. Antiquity always begets the opinion of right." "It is sufficiently understood, that the opinion of right to property, is of the greatest moment in all matters of government."

Hume's Essays.

[50]*Omnia mala exampla ex bonis initiis orta sunt.*

Sallust. Bell. Cat. S. 50.

[51]"The Republic is always attacked with greater vigour than it is defended, for the audacious and profligate, prompted by their natural enmity to it, are easily impelled to act upon the least nod of their leaders; whereas the honest, I know not why, are generally slow and unwilling to stir; and neglecting always the beginnings of things, are never roused to exert themselves, but by the last necessity; so that through irresolution and delay, when they would be glad to compound at last for their quiet, at the expence even of their honour, they commonly lose them both."

Cicero's Orat. for Sextius.

Such were the sentiments of this great and excellent man whose vast abilities, and the calamities of the time in which he lived, enabled him, by mournful experience, to form a just judgement on the conduct of the friends and enemies of liberty.

[52]Rapin's History of England.

[53]12 Car. II. Chap. 23, and 24.

[54]James II. Chap. 1, and 4.

[55]In the year of the city 428, ""*Duo singularia hæc ei viro primum contigere; prorogatio imperii non ame in ullo fucto et acta honore triumphus.*" Liv. B. 8. Chap. 23. 26.

"Had the rest of the Roman citizens imitated the example of L. Quintus, who refused to have his consulship continued to him, they had never admitted that custom of proroguing magistrates, and then the prolongation of their commands, the army had never been introduced, which very thing was at length the ruin of that commonwealth."

Machiavel's discourses, B. 3. Chap. 24.

[56]I don't know but it may be said with a good deal of reason, that a quick rotation of ministers is very desirable in Great-Britain. A minister there has a vast store of materials to work with. Long administrations are rather favourable to the reputation of a people abroad, than to their liberty.

[57]Demosthenes's 2d Philippic.

[58]Though duties by the late act are laid on some articles, on which no drawbacks are allowed, yet the duties imposed by the act, are so small, in comparison with the drawbacks that are allowed, that all the duties together will not amount to so much as the drawbacks.

[59]The expence of this board, I am informed, is between four and five thousand pounds sterling a year. The establishment of officers, for collecting the revenue of America, amounted before to seven thousand six hundred pounds per annum: and yet, says the author of "The regulation of the colonies," the whole remittance from all the taxes in the colonies, at an average of thirty years, has not amounted to one thousand nine hundred pounds a year, and in that time, seven or eight hundred pounds per annum only, have been remitted from North-America.

The smallness of the revenue arising from the duties in America, demonstrated that they were intended only as regulations of trade; and can any person be so blind to truth, so dull of apprehension in a matter of unspeakable importance to his country, as to imagine, that the board of commissioners lately established at such a charge, is instituted to assist in collecting one thousand nine hundred pounds a year, or the trifling duties imposed by the late act? Surely every man on this continent must perceive, that they are established for the care of a new system of revenue, which is but now begun.

[60]"Dira cælæno,"

Virgil, Æneid 2.

[61]It is not intended by these words to throw any reflection upon gentlemen, because they are possessed of offices; for many of them are certainly men of virtue, and lovers of their country. But supposed obligations of gratitude and honour may induce them to be silent. Whether these obligations ought to be regarded or not, is not so much to be considered by others, in the judgment they form of these gentlemen, as whether they think they ought to be regarded. Perhaps, therefore we shall act in the properest manner towards them, if we neither reproach nor imitate them. The persons meant in this letter, are the base-spirited wretches, who may endeavor to distinguish themselves, by their sordid zeal, in

defending and promoting measures, which they know, beyond all question, to be destructive to the just rights and true interests of their country. It is scarcely possible, to speak of these men with any degree of patience. It is scarcely possible to speak of them with any degree of propriety. For no words can truly describe their guilt, and meanness. But every honest man, on their being mentioned, will feel what cannot be expressed. If their wickedness did not blind them, they might perceive, along the coast of these colonies, many skeletons of wretched ambition; who after distinguishing themselves, in support of the Stamp-act, by a couragious contempt of their country, and of justice, have been left to linger out their miserable existence, without a government, collectorship, secretaryship, or any other commission to console them, as well as it could for loss of virtue and reputation—while numberless offices have been bestowed in these colonies, on people from Great-Britain, and new ones are continually invented to be thus bestowed. As a few great prizes are put into a lottery to tempt multitudes to lose, so here and there an American has been raised to a good post—

"Apparent rari nantes in gurgite vasto."

Mr. Grenville, indeed, in order to recommend the Stamp-act, had the unequalled generosity, to pour down a golden shower of offices upon Americans; and yet these ungrateful colonies did not thank Mr. Grenville for shewing his kindness to their countrymen, nor them for accepting it. How must that great statesman have been surprised to find, that the unpolished colonists could not be reconciled to infamy, by treachery? Such a bountiful disposition towards us never appeared in any minister before him, and probably never will appear again. For it is evident that such a system of policy is to be established on this continent, as, in a short time, is to render it utterly unnecessary to use the least art in order to conciliate our approbation of any measures. Some of our countrymen may be employed to fix chains upon us; but they will never be permitted to hold them afterwards. So that the utmost that any of them can expect, is only a temporary provision, that may expire in their own time; but which, they may be assured, will preclude their children from having any consideration paid to them. The natives of America, will sink into total neglect and contempt, the moment that their country loses the constitutional powers she now possesses. Most sincerely do I wish and pray, that every one of us may be convinced of this great truth, that industry and integrity are the "paths of pleasantness, which lead to happiness."

[62]Deut. vi. 7.

[63]Montesquieu's Spirit of Laws, B. 14. C. 13.

[64]*"Instrumenta regni."* Tacitus An. b. 12. s. 66.

If any person shall imagine that he discovers in these letters the least disaffection towards our most excellent Sovereign, and the parliament of Great-Britain; or the least dislike to the dependance of these colonies on that kingdom, I beg that such person will not form any judgment on particular expressions, but will consider the tenour of all the letters taken together. In that case, I flatter myself that every unprejudiced reader will be convinced, that the true interests of Great-Britain are as dear to me as they ought to be to every good subject.

If I am an Enthusiast in anything, it is in my zeal for the perpetual dependance of these colonies on their mother-country.—A dependance founded on mutual benefits, the continuance of which can be secured only by mutual affections. Therefore it is, that with extreme apprehension I view the smallest seeds of discontent, which are unwarily scattered abroad. Fifty or sixty years will make astonishing alterations in these colonies; and this consideration should render it the business of Great Britain more and more to cultivate our good dispositions towards her: but the misfortune is, that those great men, who are wrestling for power at home, think themselves very slightly interested in the prosperity of their country fifty or sixty years hence; but are deeply concerned in blowing up a popular clamour for supposed immediate advantages.

For my part, I regard Great-Britain as a bulwark happily fixed between these colonies and the powerful nations of Europe. That kingdom is our advanced post or fortification, which remaining safe, we under its protection enjoying peace, may diffuse the blessings of religion, science, and liberty, thro' remote wildernesses. It is, therefore, incontestibly our duty and our interest, to support the strength of Great Britain. When, confiding in that strength, she begins to forget from whence it arose, it will be an easy thing to shew the source. She may readily be reminded of the loud alarm spread among her merchants and tradesmen, by the universal association of these colonies, at the time of the Stamp-act, not to import any of her manufactures.——In the year 1718, the Russians and Swedes, entered into an agreement, not to suffer Great-Britain to export any naval stores from their dominions, but in Russian or Swedish ships, and at their own prices. Great-Britain was distressed. Pitch and tar rose to three pounds a barrel. At length she thought of getting these articles from the colonies; and the attempt succeeding, they fell down to fifteen shillings. In the year 1756, Great Britain was threatened with an invasion. An easterly wind blowing for six weeks, she could not man her fleet, and the whole nation was thrown into the utmost consternation. The wind changed. The American ships arrived. The fleet sailed in ten or fifteen days. There are some other reflections on this subject worthy of the most deliberate attention of the British parliament; but they are of such a nature, I do not chuse to mention them publicly. I thought I discharged my duty to my country, taking the liberty, in the year 1765, while the Stamp-Act was in suspense, of writing my sentiments to a man of the greatest influence at home, who afterwards distinguished himself by espousing our cause, in the debates concerning the repeal of that act.

[65]"Ubi imperium ad ignaros aut minus bonos pervenit; novum illud exemplum, ad dignis et idoneis, ad indignos et non idoneos transfertur."

Sall. Bed. Cat. s. 50.

Made in the USA
Middletown, DE
30 January 2020

83948004R00038